Heart of
Forgiveness

Heart of Forgiveness

A Practical Path to Healing

Madeline Ko-i Bastis

Red Wheel
Boston, MA / York Beach, ME

First published in 2003 by
Red Wheel/Weiser, LLC
York Beach, ME
With offices at:
368 Congress Street
Boston, MA 02210
www.redwheelweiser.com

Library of Congress Cataloging-in-Publication Data
Bastis, Madeline Ko-i.
    Heart of forgiveness : a practical path to healing / Madeline
Ko-i Bastis.
        p. cm.
ISBN 1-59003-027-3 (pbk.)
        1. Compassion—Religous aspects—Buddhism. 2.
Forgiveness—Religious aspects—Buddhism. 3. Healing—Religious
aspects—Buddhism. I. Title.
    BQ4360.B38 2003
    294.3'422—dc21

Typeset in Janson Text

Printed in Canada
TCP

09 08 07 06 05 04 03 02
 8 7 6 5 4 3 2 1

For my dear friend Bertha in her 90th year.

Contents

Acknowledgments

Many thanks to Robyn Heisey, Jill Rogers, Valerie Cooper, and everyone at Red Wheel/Weiser. Thank you for offering me the opportunity to explore forgiveness and to revisit the incidents in my own life that needed a bit more reflection.

May you live your lives joyfully.

Preface

Several years ago, I was browsing in a local shop and found a basket filled with pewter "stones" less than an inch long. Each tiny fragment was etched with Chinese characters on one side, with the English translation on the reverse. I began to read the inscriptions but there were so many that I gave up, closed my eyes, and randomly chose four stones. What they said would be a surprise and perhaps an inspiration for me. The four stones read: courage; patience; forgiveness; and gratitude. At first, I didn't sense a connection between them. I simply placed the talismans on my home altar and when I dusted the area, I picked up the stones, enjoying the feel of their smoothness and coolness as they lay in the palm of my hand. Then I would read the words. Sometimes it seemed that one or another of them reflected what was going on in my life, or offered encouragement.

Eventually I realized that the words were connected in a very meaningful way. For quite a while, I had been holding on to a resentment and it was difficult to let the anger go and forgive. I needed to be aware of my sense of outrage when the memory of the situation arose or when someone mentioned the guilty party's name. I had to take the resentment into my meditation and be willing to explore it. It was necessary for me to notice how my body tensed and how my stomach lurched when the wounds were reopened; how my neck became stiff and my teeth clenched and my chin jutted forward when the feeling of being wronged surfaced.

It took courage to decide to detach from the story of why I was angry, the unfairness of the situation, and dreams of revenge.

It took patience to sit through many meditation periods that weren't filled with peace, but were hard work. I wasn't ready to forgive (and certainly not to forget), and that took patience as well. I had to be willing to forgive myself for not being able to forgive. But eventually the hard work paid off, and one day, when I was concentrating on the tightness in my shoulder where the resentment resided, it vanished and I was able to forgive and wish the other person well from the bottom of my heart. Immediately I was filled with immense gratitude for my life. So I could see how courage, patience, forgiveness and gratitude were entwined.

One of the meditations that I teach is Metta (loving-kindness). The goal is to open our hearts to unconditional love. We begin with ourselves, then move on to a benefactor/mentor, a dear friend, a neutral person, and finally the "enemy," or difficult person. Eventually we radiate loving-kindness to all beings.

But this is not as easy and joyful a task as it would seem. Many of us get stuck when we try to open to unconditional love, so a forgiveness practice has been given to us. This book is based on these three forgiveness phrases:

> *For all the harm I have done to others, knowingly or unknowingly, forgive me.*
> *For all the harm others have done to me, knowingly or unknowingly, I forgive you as much as I can.*
> *For all the harm I have done myself, knowingly or unknowingly, I forgive myself.*

During my work with cancer, AIDS, psychiatric, and Alzheimer's patients; with battered women, caregivers, jail inmates, addicts, as well as so-called normal people, I have found that nothing is more difficult than forgiveness. Some people cannot ask for forgiveness, some cannot forgive another, some of us don't even realize that we are our own harshest judge and withhold forgiveness from ourselves.

In this book, we will reflect on what forgiveness really means and how it can heal our lives and relationships. We will explore the difficult emotions that keep us from forgiving and learn to work with them through meditation, guided imagery, and exercises. We will discover that a forgiving heart is a loving heart.

❧ 1 ❧

Heart of Forgiveness

Forgiveness is the final form of love.
—Rheinhold Niebuhr

It may be difficult to define forgiveness, but it is almost impossible to define love. We bandy the word about, sometimes using it to express our deepest emotion, sometimes using it lightly. A mother may say to her baby, "I love you." In the heat of a romantic tryst you whisper, "I love you." You receive a sweater for a gift and exclaim, "I love it!" The words are the same, but the meaning is different. What do you mean by love?

❧ Practice: Exploring Love ❧

Take a piece of paper and a pencil, and draw two columns. In the left column, list all the things (not people) you love. Keep going until nothing else occurs to you. In the second column, list the things you love the least.

- Can you find any similarities between the two lists?
- Why do you love one thing and not another?

In doing this exercise, you might discover that the items are just "things." What makes us love one thing and hate another is simply personal preference. You may love hard rock music and hate rap. I may love rap and hate hard rock. There is nothing especially lovable about either. So our love is conditional.

Love is also changeable. As time goes by, you may tire of rock and prefer golden oldies. If you become deaf, you may not love music at all.

A while ago, my sister and I were reminiscing and rooted out family photograph albums. As we turned the pages, we began to laugh at the clothes we had chosen to wear when we were teenagers: Lorraine in her black Capri pants, fuzzy sweater, and dangling earrings; me in a madras wrap-around skirt with round-collared blouse and circle pin. In those days, we had each thought we were the epitome of style. But over the years, our tastes had changed; we had outgrown our outfits—in more ways than one! So when we say we love something, it is not absolute.

Turn the paper over and make two new columns. Begin to list the names of people you love. Keep going as long as names pop up, but when you have to search your memory, stop. In the second column list the people you love the least (dislike, hate) until you run out of names.

Now ask yourself these questions, first about the people in column one, then in column two.

- If you borrowed money from me and never paid it back, would I forgive you?
- If you belittled me in front of my friends, would I forgive you?
- If you physically harmed me, would I forgive you?
- If you lied to me, would I forgive you?

Were you more likely to forgive those you love, or those you hate? Generally, we are more willing to forgive the people we love and who love us in return. But that love is conditional as well. You may have listed your husband, but if he divorced you, would you still love him enough to forgive him? I know two men who had been bitter rivals at work and competed against each other in sports—they were enemies, but eventually they became life-partners. Sometimes we outgrow our tolerance just as we outgrow our clothes and what is a lover's endearing trait one day becomes a grating character defect the next.

We tend to love people who meet our expectations and fulfill our desires. If a person doesn't match up with an ideal in our minds, we dismiss her or actively hate her. If the harm occurs often enough, she moves into the unloved column.

A long time ago, when I was a neophyte meditator, I became enthralled with the idea of becoming enlightened. I went to many retreats, read classic Buddhist texts and found a teacher. My thirst for enlightenment burgeoned into greed. I "wanted" so much that I browbeat my teacher. I expected him to drop everything and be available for me several times a week. I wanted him to give up his work and become a full-time teacher. Of course, I could not make him do what I wanted and my emotions vacillated between love/deference and hatred/disrespect. Eventually, I left to practice on my own. After some years, I eased into my practice and desire relaxed its grip on me. When I no longer wanted or expected anything, things fell into place and I was ready to return to my teacher and gratefully accepted what was offered. I was able to love and respect him, no matter what.

Here is what the Buddha said about loving-kindness:
As a mother would risk her life to protect her child,
her only child, Even so should one cultivate a
boundless heart with regard to all beings.

The love we are talking about is unconditional love. It exists without discrimination. Race, creed, and ethnicity don't matter. We don't have to know a person or like him or understand him. It is not a negotiation: "You do this for me and I will love you." It is all-embracing and accepting.

Love is an expression of the connection between all beings. The names, faces and circumstances change, but at the core we are all one. Try this meditation to arouse the feeling of unconditional love and to radiate it to all beings.

❋ Practice: Awakening Loving-Kindness ❋

Quiet your mind by focusing on the feeling of your breath going in and out. It may be helpful to close your eyes. Begin by sending loving-kindness to yourself:

May I be safe from harm.
May I be free from mental suffering.
May I be free from physical suffering.
May I live my life joyfully.

Repeat the phrases several times, and then visualize your family, friends, and colleagues and send loving-kindness to them:

As I wish myself to be safe from harm, so I wish you to be safe.
May you be free from mental suffering.
May you be free from physical suffering.
May you live your lives joyfully.

Extend the loving-kindness further, to those you don't know:

May all beings—
those who I know, those who I've never met;
those who are like me, those who differ in race, religion,
    ethnicity;
those who have done good, those who have done ill—

May you be safe from harm.
May you be free from mental suffering.
May you be free from physical suffering.
May you live your lives joyfully.

Try to visualize all beings joined in a circle of mutual love and harmony, and hold the image for a few moments as you breathe in and out.

When we experience love in this way we can forgive any harm.

What Is Harm?

Before we can forgive, we need to understand what needs to be forgiven. The phrases we'll be working with begin with: "For all the harm…" What is harm?

Some religions have commandments that tell us what to avoid. They are called sins. Each nation has a list of things that are illegal. They are called crimes. Each municipality has traffic conventions. They are called regulations. Almost every group has guidelines for members. They are called rules. Families agree on appropriate behavior. They may be called boundaries.

We try to live in community without stepping on one another's toes. Keeping track of all the sins, crimes, regulations, rules, and boundaries can overwhelm us. If we aren't mindful, we're bound to cross one line or another and hurt someone.

We can be guided by the Ten Commandments of the Judeo-Christian canon or the Ten Grave Precepts of Buddhism, or try to avoid the seven sins of anger, covetousness, envy, gluttony, lust, pride, and sloth. We can abide by the laws of our country, neighborhood, clubs, and families.

But we're working with forgiveness in a personal way.

Let's look at our thoughts, words, and actions through a single lens and ask the question: Do they cause suffering?

Harm is any thought, word, or action that causes suffering in ourselves or others.

Guidelines for Awareness and Prevention of Harm

Although there are many ways to categorize harm, I'd like to view it by reflecting on five of the grave precepts that I was given when I was ordained as a Buddhist priest. I particularly like the way they are worded. They do not exhort: Do not…! They simply label the ideals to which we aspire in order not to cause suffering.

Harm is any thought, word, or action that
causes suffering in ourselves or others.

Not Killing

Most societies agree that we should avoid killing another human being. This arises from the intuitive knowledge that we are all connected, that all of life is sacred. To kill another human being is to kill a part of ourselves and to compromise the integrity of life. Each time someone is killed, it's like a moth chewing a hole in the fabric of life. The more holes there are, the weaker the fabric becomes.

Not killing includes any kind of physical harm to
people and all living creatures, as well as psychological
damage. It's possible to kill a person's spirit.

I know a woman who is paralyzed by perfectionism. When she was a child, her parents constantly told her she was not good enough, that she would never succeed, that she was a failure. She responded by becoming an overachiever—trying to win their love. That didn't work, because more and more was demanded of her. Now, as an adult, she cannot commit to any long-term project because she believes that no matter how hard she tries, her efforts will never be enough. She believes she is wasting her life. Her spirit has been killed.

Not killing doesn't just mean avoidance, it means expressing our gratitude for life by actively nurturing everything around us—the animate and inanimate. We cherish our homes, gardens, and neighborhood; we nurture the spirits of our family, friends, and neighbors. The concern extends to the entire universe; we take care of pollution, famine, war, disease, and homelessness. Nothing is outside our realm because it is all a part of us. We accept our role in keeping the fabric of life whole and strong.

Not Stealing

This is pretty clear: We don't take things that don't belong to us. I have always thought of myself as an honest person and would probably say that I've never stolen anything. Upon reflection, however, I realize that it is not so. When I was an employee, I took paper clips and pencils home, and when I ran a successful business, I allowed my accountant to use every loophole to lower my taxes.

Not stealing becomes more subtle as we reflect on it. It includes not taking that which is not offered. Once, I was on a long retreat and my job was to put away leftover food after meals. Usually the kitchen is off-limits to retreat participants but, because of my job, I was in and out all the time. We were allowed to eat as much food as we wanted during meals, and even to save some things for snacks later. One morning, I noticed that someone had a wedge of lemon in his tea. Suddenly, I wanted lemon, too, but there were no lemons in the fruit basket at breakfast, and I was frustrated. My throat felt a bit sore and I could almost taste the tart, sweet flavor of lemon and honey in my tea. I imagined how soothing the tea would feel as it slid down my throat. There was a large bowl of lemons in the kitchen and I rationalized that I could take one. Perhaps I would leave money for it. Visions of lemons haunted my meditation.

The next day I awoke to the image of lemons. I knew I shouldn't take one, but the temptation was strong. Finally, in desperation, I asked the cook to give me a lemon. And she did!

I didn't have to steal or borrow; all I had to do was ask. The cook could not intuit what I wanted, she needed to be told. In this way, I learned that

> *Part of not stealing is being able to ask for*
> *and graciously accept what is needed.*

There is enough for everyone. Generosity in sharing my own resources is part of the precept as well. In addition to material things like money and time, I can share my spiritual wealth as well—offering encouragement, mindful listening, and kind words.

Not Being Greedy

This applies to sexual conduct. We understand that sex is communion between two people. In its most sublime form, there is no giver, no receiver, only the act of love.

> *We do not seek to assuage our own*
> *desire at the expense of another.*

This means generosity within the act itself, but also taking care not to harm another. So although the precept doesn't explicitly prohibit pre- or extra-marital sex, it does remind us that we must be aware of the feelings of others before we act to slake our desire. Is there a spouse, lover, or friend who will be hurt if we act? Are we breaking a promise? Are we threatening a relationship?

When we choose a partner on the spur of the moment, are we just using him because he's available? Is there mutual caring?

When we are in a committed relationship, are we demanding or clinging? Do we make love a negotiation instead of a gift? The precept helps to make us aware that there is more to love than just sex.

Although this precept is sometimes called "not misusing sex," we understand that the underlying motive is self-centered greed. So not being greedy also encompasses relationships. Sometimes our neediness masquerades as love, and genuine affection becomes warped by jealousy, obsessive clinging, or controlling behavior. In other settings we may strive to be the favorite child, the teacher's pet, or the boss's right hand man.

Not Lying

We like to think that we are truthful, but sometimes the line between truth and falsehood is blurred. I have a friend who lived in an exotic land for several years when she was young. She fell in love with a fellow student who happened to be distantly related to the ruling family. When she returned home, she told her friends that she had been swept off her feet by a prince. It may have felt that way, but the truth was that he was not a prince. She told the romantic tale many, many times, and after a while, she believed the story was true.

Each of us has embellished our life experiences in some way. Real life seems to be a black-and-white movie and we crave Technicolor. This kind of lying comes from a need to be special; its inverse is false humility.

During Zen training, one of the teacher's jobs is to dismantle the student's ego. The final goal is for the student to experience selflessness, which paradoxically leads to a feeling of unity with all beings. In this state, there is no need to be special, because we realize that all of us are special. Although each of us is unique, we share the same perfect essence. There is no lack, nothing extra. That's the goal, but sometimes it doesn't happen that way.

I have always been a capable, organized person who learns new tasks quickly. I had a fair amount of pride in this, which my teachers sought to crumble. During work practice at a Buddhist monastery, I was never allowed to be in charge of a group or to work on projects that drew on my expertise and experience, such as gardening, graphic design, or bookkeeping. I spent much of my time cleaning bathrooms and preparing bulk mailings. Occasionally, they would give me a new task, something that was completely alien to me. Once I was enlisted to tape and spackle a newly-renovated office. At first, I was clumsy, but eventually I got the hang of it and enjoyed the work. The contractor began to tell people how good I was at the job and the next day my teacher "demoted" me to mowing the lawn.

Another teacher constantly told me I was too proud and humiliated me whenever possible. As a result, I became self-deprecating. When I was a chaplain intern, it was difficult for me to acknowledge that I was doing a good job. My supervisor picked up the shattered pieces of my ego and my new practice became owning my triumphs without excessive pride and admitting my failures without shame.

When there is awareness and acceptance
of self and others, there is no need to lie.

We may lie to avoid punishment or embarrassment, but more frequently, we lie in order to get what we want. Sometimes the purpose behind a lie is to hurt another. In all instances, we lie because we are not happy with the way things are.

Whenever one of my college buddies was disappointed, she'd say, *"C'est la vie."* It seemed trite at the time, but after years of meditation practice, I realize the wisdom of that old saw. "That's life" is not so different from the Buddhist teaching of "things are as they are."

Not Clouding the Mind

At the end of sitting meditation, Zen students frequently chant the Four Great Vows and the second one is: "Reality is boundless, I vow to perceive it." We declare our willingness to become aware of and accept everything around us, because we intuitively understand that everything is as it should be. There is no need to ignore, avoid, or water down our experience. We don't have to cloud our minds with excessive alcohol or drugs. Nowadays there are additional possibilities for clouding the mind: obsessive attachment to television, video games, and the Internet. What we are doing is trying to escape into a fantasy world of daydreams.

The flip side of escapism is a zest for life, no matter what is happening. As one Zen teacher said: "Be here now." This is it. The good times and the bad, the wins and losses make up our lives.

Be present; embrace your life.

In addition to the big five precepts, there are two others that I particularly like.

Not Talking about Others' Errors and Faults

We all ignore this one. Gossip is a pop-culture phenomenon fed by tabloids, weekly magazines, and "inside information" TV shows. Because of the rampant gossip that we see and hear everyday, we tend to think it's all right to talk about people's faults. There is a measure of glee to think that a person is not perfect and so it's easy to be drawn into backbiting. There is a natural tendency to blame and criticize others when things don't go the way we think they should.

A friend of mine had a high-powered job with a large staff. He was good about delegating responsibility, but a little lax about asking for updates from his team. One large deal was not completed because the project manager dropped the ball. John fumed and worried and placed the blame on the manager. John didn't acknowledge that he was responsible for his entire staff.

When we realize that we are not victims
we can accept responsibility for our actions
and not resort to blame.

Not Elevating Yourself by Putting Down Others

Most of us share an impulse to feel important and special. One way to shore up shaky self-esteem is to brag about our accomplishments. In this there is a subtle message: I am better than you. We go about our lives as if we were in a competition, hoping to climb one step higher on a ladder. When someone gets ahead of us, we may try to belittle what they have done.

Once, when a group of us was practicing chants for a

Buddhist service, Rose suggested that she ask Mark, who had a wonderful basso profundo voice, to instruct her. I replied that he liked the sound of his voice too much. I have a sub-par singing voice, and I had belittled Mark's accomplishment by implying that he was proud and arrogant. A few days later, I heard that Rose had told not only Mark, but several others including the head priest. I had elevated myself, and then Rose had elevated herself by speaking of my faults and it began a chain of anger and resentment.

We do not see that there are no winners or losers. Each of us has gifts that can be celebrated without taking away anything from ourselves.

Why Do We Cause Harm?

At Zen retreats, before dawn meditation we chant this verse:

All evil karma, ever committed by me since of old,
On account of my beginningless greed, anger and ignorance,
Born of my body, mouth and thought,
Now I atone for it all.

> *The three poisons of greed, anger, and ignorance*
> *are the root causes of harmful thoughts, words,*
> *and actions. Each of these qualities arises because*
> *we are not comfortable with the way things are.*

Greed/Attachment

Greed, which includes desire, is a deep longing for more. It comes from a belief that we are not sufficient unto ourselves. We feel a fundamental lack in our worth and think that if we accumulate wealth, power, love, or fame we will be happy. When we do achieve some of these things, we fiercely cling to them, fearing they will disappear. Our attachment becomes neurotic and we spend our time protecting what we have amassed and planning how to get more. In the course of accumulating and protecting, we begin to cause harm to ourselves and others. To get what we desire we may lie, cheat, steal, or kill. We may become overly competitive and constantly compare ourselves to others. So we seesaw between pride and self-doubt.

Anger/Aversion

Anger is another response to challenging circumstances. Things are not going the way we think they should and we become angry. We try to get rid of what is bothering us. We lash out against others by shouting, fighting, killing. Subtler responses are belittling, backbiting, undercutting, and sabotage. We may react in a different, no less damaging way, by turning the anger inward and becoming depressed and withdrawn, or turn to alcohol or drugs to drown our discontent.

Ignorance/Delusion

The ignorance we're speaking of is the lack of understanding that there is no separate self. Everything that we think of as our self—our bodies, minds, jobs, things—is ephemeral. There is no one thing we can point to as "me." Imagine that you are a balloon filled with air. The air inside and the air outside are the same. When the balloon is pricked, there is just air. Until we burst the balloon, we float around at the mercy of breezes and storms. We are bewildered and may cause harm to ourselves or others, because we haven't realized that we are one with the universe. Harming another is really harming ourselves.

Fear

Fear is the seed; the three poisons are the fruit. We fear that we will not get what we want or lose what we already have—desire. We fear that difficult circumstances will not change and so react—anger. We fear that we are isolated—ignorance.

Although everyone acts out of greed, anger, or ignorance at some time or other, most of us fall into one of the major categories. Desire and attachment can rule our lives, or we can be angry and judgmental because nothing satisfies us. We may live in confusion, not understanding our place in the universe, fecklessly disregarding the consequences for ourselves and others. Each of us has a propensity for a particular poison. There is a personal character as well as family and national characters. As we delve into forgiveness, it's helpful to realize that all harm stems from one of the three poisons. We can always trace the motives to attachment, aversion, or delusion.

So when you are harmed or you harm others, look carefully to discover the root cause.

Thoughts, Words, and Actions

When I was in the fourth grade at St. Sylvester's Elementary School, the class spent most of the term preparing for our first Holy Communion. Most of us didn't grasp the import of the occasion, but we girls were excited about getting to wear flouncy white dresses and filmy veils. We would receive presents, too—new rosary beads, a prayer book, a lace-edged handkerchief in a white plastic purse. On the momentous day, we would also get to carry a bouquet. I remember that mine was composed of red sweetheart roses surrounded by a scalloped doily. But before we could take part in the exciting day, we had to study our catechism and prepare for our first confession. I remember that we had to look at how we had sinned in thought, word, and deed—thought, mouth, and body.

Greed, anger, and ignorance result in harmful thoughts, words, and actions. The first harmful thought is insidious and eventually will harden into a habit of mind. We then become prisoners of our conditioned responses, doomed to repeat harmful actions and reap the consequences of negative karma.

Karma

Physicists tell us that for every action there is an equal, but opposite reaction. The Bible exhorts that you reap what you sow. The law of karma reminds us that harmful thoughts, words, and actions don't take place in a vacuum. There are endless repercussions, and in some mysterious way, our lives are changed forever. This applies to the perpetrator as well as the victim. It applies to the individual and to society as a whole. A cycle of harm is perpetuated. A teenager is baited and humiliated by peers, he is overwhelmed by anger and retaliates by shooting up the cafeteria. Students die and their parents are destroyed by grief and demand vengeance. In the following months, other schools see similar incidents.

How can we stop a spiraling descent into fear and violence? Forgiveness is the first step. We see that all of us are capable of acting from greed, anger, and ignorance, and then we forgive the sinner, not the act.

In the following pages, we'll explore the ways in which we harm ourselves and others and discover that we can break the cycle of harm by forgiving.

*Just one act of forgiveness can change our
lives and pervade the whole universe.*

❧ 2 ❧

Seeking Forgiveness

For all the harm I have done to others,
knowingly or unknowingly, forgive me.

The most surprising part of our aspiration "For all the harm I have done to others, knowingly or unknowingly, forgive me" is "knowingly or unknowingly." Major transgressions stand out in our minds, but much of the time, we are oblivious to the harm we do. How often do we make a snide remark behind someone's back or spread gossip? Do we think twice when we step on a bug or toss an aluminum can into the regular trash instead of the recycling bin? When we neglect to correct a clerk who has given us too much change do we stop to think of the repercussions—that she may be forced to work overtime to reconcile the receipts and then make up the difference from her own pocket; that she might miss her usual train and so be late in picking up her child from school; that the child is left to stand on a darkening street wondering if mom forgot him?

This line of thinking seems obsessive and picky, but it reminds us that most of us live our lives blissfully unaware of the affect we have on the people and things around us. We are like kings and queens of our realms, expecting everything to revolve around us.

But that's not the way it is. More than 2,500 years ago, a young man sat under a tree. He had taken a vow not to move from that spot until he became enlightened. He entered a deep state of meditation and all of his past lives came into his consciousness. He was tempted by the forces of evil to forsake his vow. He was offered beautiful women and power, and experienced terrifying visions. Still, he did not leave his seat. When dawn broke and he gazed at the morning sun, it was as if he was seeing it for the first time, and he attained enlightenment.

What did he find out? He saw that there is no separate self; everything is connected. It is what the Vietnamese Zen teacher Thich Nhat Hahn calls "interbeing."

The young man was from then on called the Buddha, the awakened one.

Sharpening Awareness

The first step for us is to wake up to what we are doing.

The best way to do this is to quiet the chattering mind that is forever planning, daydreaming, remembering, and judging, and return to the still point that is the real center of the universe—the present moment.

> *Do you have the patience to wait*
> *till your mud settles and the water is clear?*
> —*Tao Te Ching*, Verse 15,
> Stephen Mitchell, trans.

❀ Practice: Quieting the Mind ❀

Find a quiet spot and decide to sit still for five minutes. Close your eyes and watch your breath carefully, labeling the inhalation as "in" and the exhalation as "out." When you notice your mind wandering, simply note "thinking," and return to watching your breath. After a time, you may want to count the exhalations from one through ten, then start over again. Don't be harsh with yourself if you lose count. Simply note "thinking" and begin again at number one.

It may seem odd to try to stop the mind from thinking when we wish to sharpen awareness, because our normal way is to do as much as possible in the shortest time span. Sometimes I eat dinner in front of the TV, while glancing at my mail, and when the phone rings, I answer it. Am I really tasting the food, hearing the news, understanding the mail, and paying attention to the conversation? Focusing on one thing at a time allows our racing minds to settle and become as clear as a pristine mountain lake. The mud settles to the bottom and the surface becomes flat, like a mirror.

Just as a still lake reflects the surrounding landscape, our still mind allows us to clearly see our habits and how we act in the world.

The more often we take the time to quiet the mind, the more we learn about ourselves. Sometimes the discovery is not pleasant.

During my first week-long meditation retreat, I was sitting, counting my breaths. Of course, I had to note "thinking" a million times, and start again at number one. I thought I never would be able to get to ten more than twice in a row. Slowly but steadily, annoyance nibbled at my concentration because things were not going the way I had planned. Wasn't the point of going on retreat to feel peaceful and serene and perhaps even get enlightened? Annoyance escalated to frustration until I felt ready to explode. Everything disintegrated—my legs fell asleep and my back ached. When it was time for my interview with the teacher, I waited in line a long time, and then the bell rang, signaling the end of interviews and I resentfully skulked back to my seat to wait a few more hours. At night, I couldn't sleep because of tension and, as a result, during the day my mind was groggy. I didn't like the food and the meditation hall was too noisy because someone was coughing. I felt short-changed and the desire to leap up from the cushion and run from the meditation hall became unbearable. Then, a moment of clarity dawned and I realized that this was the way I always lived my life. When things didn't go the way I wanted them to, I was out of there!

This insight was not what I had expected, but it proved to be a treasure. I had experienced one cause of suffering in my own life: anger when things were unpleasant and desire to escape.

I realized that when I got angry it was usually at someone who was not acting the way I thought she or he should, and then I would either act out (fight) or erase her or him from my life with no explanation (flight). Most of the time these were knee-jerk reactions that occurred automatically. Years of mindless repetition had created habits that dictated how I lived in the world. I had no freedom because my responses were programmed. I had turned into an angry, contentious, self-centered person. It was a hard pill to swallow.

Acceptance

My self-esteem was built on a faulty foundation, and when I saw clearly how I really was, my inflated sense of self-worth plummeted. I had hated everyone else and now I hated myself as well. Each time I sat in meditation, ways in which I had been hurtful to others arose and my depression deepened. I believed I was a terrible person.

Even though we may not like to admit it, most of us feel this way at some time in our lives. We become mired in self-loathing. But this stuckness is a blessing.

Here is a Zen koan:
When you reach the top of a hundred-foot
pole, how do you move forward?

When you cannot move forward or backward; when you no longer can maintain footing on the tip of the pole; what do you do? The only answer is to surrender. For me it was to learn to accept all sides of myself, both the good and the bad.

At this time in my life, I had been attending self-help meetings. Although I had been in recovery from alcohol abuse for five years, I had not really followed any of the group's suggestions. But I was ready to give up. I asked a twenty-year veteran to help me with a "fearless and searching moral inventory," the fourth in A. A.'s Twelve Steps program. M. agreed, and we met once a week during the summer. She is wise as well as strong and as I listed my bad points, M. gently suggested that I remember my good points as well. At the end of the summer, we filled in a balance sheet and I found that my positive traits slightly edged out the negative ones. Ah! There is light at the end of the tunnel.

❦ Practice: Taking Stock of Your Actions ❦

When you are ready, begin to make your own list. Draw two columns on a page. Label the left column "Dark" and the right column "Light," or create your own headings. (One student drew frowning and happy faces; another used "Negative" and "Positive.") Under "Dark," write down an action that caused harm to another. On the "Light" side, list something that helped another. Don't write anything in the dark column again until you have discovered something positive that you have done.

You can continue this practice during one sitting, but it may be helpful to keep an ongoing journal. Whenever you become aware of harming someone, write it down and then sit quietly, following your breath and ask yourself: What have I done today to help another? There will be something, trust me.

Start the list with actions, but as your awareness sharpens, you can include harmful thoughts as well.

Writing down what I perceived to be "bad" about my actions along with what were "good" helped me see that they formed the warp and weft of my personality. They were integral to the tapestry of my life, and each trait was colored by its opposite. For example, my ability to get things done quickly sometimes led me to be impatient with others. My generosity with time and help sometimes made people feel inept. On the other hand, sometimes my criticism sparked positive change in a person. None of the traits was wholly positive or negative on its own. It depended on how the trait manifested. As one of my teachers noted, "It's not what you say, Madeline, but how you say it."

I had awakened to the various facets of my personality, had formed a truce with them, but now it was time for action. I needed to step off the hundred-foot pole. I had to learn to love them.

Befriending

When I lived in Manhattan, I used to walk my dog Daisy in Central Park. One Sunday afternoon, as we entered at 96th Street, I noticed a small, shaggy dog tied to the fence. She was mewling and had no collar or nametag. I hoped that her owner had left her for a few minutes and would return, but after a couple of hours, when I was leaving the park, the dog was still there. I was torn—I couldn't bear to leave her, but on the other hand, two dogs in a tiny apartment was not an option. I went home but my conscience wouldn't let me rest so I went back to the park to rescue her. I planned to find a home for her if no one responded to the signs I had posted in the park. When I brought her to a vet to check out her health, I mentioned that she would be easy to place because she was so cute. The vet laughed, saying that many people were drawn to the scruffiest dogs, some of them maimed and ill.

It is possible to look at our ourselves and see the part of us that is maimed and scruffy and love it.

When I attended my first Metta retreat, the idea of wishing myself well seemed outrageous. I was there to practice loving other people. But there was a sequence to be followed and I, ever the good student, got with the program. For several days, I envisioned myself and repeated the phrases, "May I love myself exactly as I am. May I be happy with things just as they are." It sounded hokey and at first, I was embarrassed, but after eight days of practice, my relationship to myself changed for the better and, not coincidentally, my relationship to others improved as well.

🎋 Practice: Befriending Yourself 🎋

Sit quietly and begin by watching your breath for a few moments.

Connect with your body by noticing your feet touching the floor, or the weight of your hands in your lap. Then visualize yourself. Inhale and exhale, then silently say the phrase:

May I love myself exactly as I am.

Inhale and exhale, then say:

May I be happy with things just as they are.

Inhale, exhale:

May I love myself exactly as I am.

Inhale, exhale:

May I be happy with things just as they are.

Keep repeating this phrase for several minutes. If you notice your attention drifting, recall the image of yourself, inhale, exhale, and then continue repeating the phrases. As you do this practice, you may notice an inner voice whispering that you don't deserve love; that you are a bad person. Memories of harmful actions may come up. Acknowledge them, perhaps silently saying, "I'm sorry," then return to the breath and the phrases.

This practice may seem repetitious, but we're expressing a heartfelt wish to love all parts of ourselves. Perhaps other phrases will occur to you. That's okay. Just remember to frame them with "May I..." which expresses a willingness to receive. An affirmation such as "I am...." has a strident, defiant tone; proclaiming something that you don't fully believe. Loving-kindness practice is meant to open our hearts, to break through the wall of defenses we have built to protect ourselves from being wounded. It is meant to make us vulnerable, both to our own hurts and the hurts we have inflicted on others. And this softness may lead to regret.

Remorse

When we quiet the mind, our transgressions emerge from the shadows and we become sensitive to our interaction with others. A turning point presents itself. Though we feel regret at having caused harm, there may still be a niggling voice whispering that our actions were necessary. Tit for tat; he deserved that; we were not acting, only reacting. It's important to remember that we alone are in control of our actions. When the words and actions of other people dictate our choices, we are not free. This is our opportunity to make a major change in our lives and unyoke ourselves from the ingrained habit of being reactive.

We acknowledge our responsibility for our own thoughts and actions and feel regret for causing suffering. The remorse is deep and genuine, because we realize that when we harm others, we harm ourselves. We are all connected—interbeing.

When I felt this overwhelming remorse, I decided to apologize to the people I may have hurt with my angry words or gestures. Because I had probably harmed hundreds over my lifetime, it was impossible to remember them all, much less ask for forgiveness. But it is willingness that's important, so I decided to start with the people I did remember.

This is where courage came in. It's fairly easy to say "I'm sorry" a few minutes or days after an argument, but much more difficult after months or years. That required humility. Looking into my heart, I realized that my intention to apologize was paramount. I was seeking forgiveness not to make myself feel better, but to bear witness to the harm I may have done to others. Because I couldn't locate or even recall every person who deserved an apology, I remembered my Catholic childhood and for the first time in 25 years, I decided to go to confession.

It was a momentous event. The day was suitably dreary and a heavy mist had settled on the grass surrounding the church. I had called ahead to make sure a priest would be present and had reviewed the sins I had committed and planned to make a general confession. To my surprise, there was no longer a private booth. I sat face-to-face with a priest and began with tears in my eyes,

"Forgive me father for I have sinned. It has been 25 years since my last confession."

The priest interrupted, "That's okay, God will forgive you. Just kneel at the altar and say you're sorry." He then gave absolution.

I was shocked—not even a rosary for penance! It had taken years to realize that I had indeed caused harm and months to summon up the humility to ask for forgiveness. The priest was not prepared to listen. Perhaps it was boredom, or perhaps an act of kindness on his part, but the great release I had hoped for was denied.

Even though I was sorry for hurting people, there was still the underlying desire to free myself of the burden of guilt and shame. Some self-help programs suggest that we share our sins before God and another human being. I remember an older woman who had a slogan ready for every situation. One was, "It's better to cry and share it, than grin and bear it." It does feel better to share grief and anger and guilt. When I was doing research about forgiveness on the Internet, I found several confession sites. People could e-mail their sins to the site where the entire narrative would be posted for anyone to read. There is a need to unburden guilt, even to unknown strangers.

At first, I wondered why people would read the confessions. Some people probably enjoyed the vicarious thrill of sharing secrets, but others, I thought, wanted to feel a connection with others. We're all in the same boat and share the same faults and foibles.

But

> *True remorse comes from a sense*
> *of oneness with all beings.*

We wish to seek forgiveness not to make ourselves feel better, but to acknowledge that we have caused suffering for another.

We're not always able to make amends to everyone. We lose touch, we forget names, or people have died. But it is possible to acknowledge our remorse.

❊ Practice: Expressing Remorse ❊

Decide to walk in a natural setting that you enjoy—the woods, countryside, or shore. Guilt has been locked inside for so long that it is helpful to release it to the four directions. Find a place to sit and begin to watch your breath. Open to the sounds around you—leaves murmuring in the wind, waves spanking the shore, insects humming by. Begin to picture each person you have hurt, and say silently:

For all the harm I have done to you, knowingly
  or unknowingly, forgive me.
As I wish myself to be happy, so I wish you to be happy.
May your life be filled with joy and well-being.

Keep repeating the words until you feel a loosening in your heart. Then move on to another person.

It can take many outings to ask forgiveness of the people we have caused to suffer. It may be easier to start with small transgressions. When you feel as if you have released some guilt, then make a symbolic gesture: releasing a balloon, tossing a stone into the ocean, blowing out a candle.

Words alone may not suffice.

Atonement

The usual definition of atonement is making amends. But before we can make amends, we need to fully comprehend what we have done, both how it feels for us to harm and how it feels for the other to be harmed. It is called at-one-ment. We become intimate with our thoughts and actions. Most of us like to skip over this part, because it's difficult. But

> *We cannot truly make amends until we experience*
> *the pain we have caused ourselves and others.*

🎇 Practice: At-one-ment 🎇

Sit quietly and begin to watch your breath. When you feel as if your mind has settled, then recall the incident that caused harm.

Inhale, exhale and ask yourself:

Why did I act that way?

Was the motivation fear, or anger, or jealousy, or lust, or greed? When you think you have an answer, then try to access the emotion. Notice where in your body the emotion settles. It could be a knot in your stomach, a tightening in the shoulders, gritted teeth, constriction around your heart.

Inhale, exhale, and place all of your attention on the sensation.

Notice if it's large or small, strong or weak, tingling or

stabbing or throbbing.

What color is the emotion? Focus on the color and see what happens.

Does the color remain the same or does it change?

Does it vibrate or remain static?

Does it become more or less intense?

Does it metamorphose into another color?

Does it fade away?

When the sensation and color seem to dissipate, clear your mind and return to your breath.

Call to mind the image of the person you have harmed. Imagine how the person must have felt when you wounded them. Call up the emotion and notice where it appears in your body. Investigate the sensation and notice if it changes.

This is one way to become intimate with our transgressions. We become at one with our victim's feelings as well as our own. In this intimacy, this walking in another's shoes, we come to see that we all feel the same things. You may discover that the emotions that motivated you to harm are identical to the feelings of being harmed. This insight offers opportunity to change the way we act when we are angry, fearful, or greedy. That's true at-one-ment.

Making Amends

Making amends may not be as simple as apologizing, paying back stolen money, or correcting an exaggeration or lie.

When my graphic design business in Manhattan was in its infancy, I hired my first full-time employee. After interviewing several people, I settled on Andy who seemed to have a cheerful, upbeat personality. He would need it, because in previous jobs, I had a reputation for being a driven, difficult boss. We worked together for several years and although I was a control freak, Andy began to wrest more and more responsibility from me until he was doing the billing and bookkeeping. He insisted that I buy expensive equipment that quickly helped turn a larger profit. His warm personality helped client relations, and the business began to flourish. Although I often mentioned to clients that Andy was in a large measure responsible for our success, I never thanked him.

Andy didn't have a sister and he invited me to fill that role. Because I was wrapped up in my own sense of isolation, I ignored his outstretched arms.

After I sold the business to Andy and moved to Long Island, he would call every few days to update me on new projects at work or the imminent move to larger offices. Each triumph reminded me that I was not indispensable and I greeted his news not with joy but with cynicism. Not coincidentally, I was drinking heavily at the time. Gradually the calls became further apart until they stopped altogether.

A couple of years later, his secretary called to tell me that Andy had died from pneumonia, a result of AIDS. He hadn't told me he was sick, and rightly so, because at that time I was too self-centered to be of any help.

I was filled with remorse and self-loathing. There was a snowstorm on the day of his funeral and the bus I rode into the city was very late. As I entered the funeral home, the mourners were leaving and the casket was being carried out. Again, I had failed Andy.

As time passed, the memory of the incident faded. I was newly sober, had started a garden design business, and had just begun Zen practice. But all of our failures are stored in the dark recesses of our minds, waiting to emerge.

In 1992 I entered training as a hospital chaplain at a cancer hospital in Manhattan. At first, I was not very good at it, being introverted and self-conscious. I formed relationships with patients who themselves were outgoing. One handsome Greek American was felled by leukemia in the prime of life. His business was successful, his daughter was engaged to be married, and he had recently attained his dream of owning a large sailboat. He was so full of *joie de vivre* and brimming with energy that he and his family were confident that he would beat the disease. A few months later, that changed. When I walked into his room, I almost didn't recognize the pale, wasted man who was in great pain. His charm was still there and the undercurrent of sadness made it all the more compelling. As I held his hand and we talked, he finally asked me, "Madeline, what made you do this work? Are you doing penance for something?" I was taken aback and said I wished to learn more about pain and suffering, but later, as I reflected on his question, I knew that he had seen what I had not yet glimpsed.

My favorite patients were usually men with AIDS (like Andy) or cancer patients (like my father). The vocation to my new ministry came from a deep longing in my heart for atonement. Subconsciously, I knew I had to make amends for abandoning Andy and sought a second chance to help my father better when he died. Chaplaincy was my solution.

From that moment on, my ministry blossomed because there was no longer any pressure to do things perfectly, to be all things to all people, or to make up for what had happened in the past. I was no longer trying to create the intimacy that I had rejected years ago. I no longer tried to make every AIDS patient into a surrogate Andy. I was free to do what needed to be done, without expecting patients to become attached to me. Just like a firefighter. When there's a fire, you put it out. You don't go back day after day expecting thanks for the job you did. You go on to the next fire.

You can make amends to people you have harmed, too. If there is someone to whom you wish to make amends, and they are not available because you have lost touch or they have died, there are still ways to atone. There is a phrase from the Old Testament, "An eye for an eye; a tooth for a tooth," which is about payback and revenge. But there's another way to look at it.

If you cannot make amends directly, a sincere
search will reveal the path to at-one-ment.

✿ Practice: Making Amends ✿

Make a list of people to whom you would like to make amends. Write down their names, and how you harmed them. If any of the people are available, write down the appropriate action to express your regret. For example, if you have lied about a person, then correct it. If the person is not reachable, then think of an alternate way to atone for your words or actions. Here are some examples:

If you have stolen money or left a loan unpaid, then make restitution to the family. If you cannot find them, then donate money to charity.

If you have spoken words of hate about an ethnic group, resolve to learn more about their heritage to understand them.

If you have polluted the environment by tossing toxic items in the regular trash, then adopt a road and pick up litter.

If you have lied about someone, resolve to tell the truth in the future.

Apologizing Face-to-Face

We might be willing to admit that we have caused harm, but meeting the person face-to-face to make an apology is difficult. It takes courage to own up to our faults and humility to acknowledge them to another. Although we know that after the apology we will feel relieved and that it is a step toward reconciliation, it is a scary thing to do. Sometimes we wimp out and make a phone call or send a funny card, but true remorse requires more.

> *To look the person in the eyes and express*
> *sincere regret will help us to think before we*
> *act the next time a similar situation occurs.*

The way we apologize is significant. Sometimes there is no true remorse, only a desire to relieve guilt.

When I was a garden designer, an acquaintance from a self-help group asked me to give some advice and an estimate for a reflecting pool. Usually, I require a consultation fee and a down payment before I set foot on a property. Because I knew this man, I let that formality slide. I spent several hours giving him my ideas and measuring the property. Then I invested more time doing sketches and preparing a detailed estimate. He didn't return my phone calls, and later I found that he had hired someone else to install my design. Finally, he called and said, "I'm sorry to have taken up your time; enough said." Then he hung up. Clearly, he had called out of a sense of duty and to make himself feel better. He had lived up to the letter of the step of admitting his fault, but the spirit was missing. Whenever I ran into him, he avoided my eyes.

For my part, the half-hearted apology rankled more than the act itself.

If it is impossible for you face the person you hurt, then write a letter. You may need to write several drafts, until you get the tone right. Try to concentrate on assuaging the other person's feelings, rather than justifying your actions. Humility is the key.

Every year I lead several weekend retreats and all the advertising, registration forms, travel directions, special food needs, and room requests are funneled through one phone line. Some people enroll early and then change their minds; others call at the last minute when there's no time to prepay and then don't show up. The retreat house requires constant updates on the number of participants. Leading the retreat is the easy part; handling the picky details is grueling.

The day before one retreat, a woman called to say that she couldn't attend because a friend had just been admitted to hospice and she didn't want to leave her. This woman had made many calls about the details of the retreat, and I suspected the truth of her story. I was annoyed and was testy on the phone. After I had hung up, I realized that I had been rude, noted it, but the business of the retreat drove it from my mind.

Several days later I received this note:

Dear Madeline:

I could not help but hear your annoyance and possible disbelief when I called the other morning to say I would not be able to make the retreat. Perhaps you thought I decided not to come because my sister was unable to fly up for the weekend. In any case I just wanted you to know that I made the right decision to stay back. I have enclosed my friend's obituary and as you can see she passed away on Friday evening [the first day of the retreat]. I am home from work today preparing to attend her funeral service. I must say considering the retreat was going to be focused on meditation for healing I was surprised by your response. It would have been nice if you had thought to offer some kind words of understanding. I am sorry for any difficulty my canceling may have caused you.

Sincerely,

L.

You can imagine my feeling of chagrin. My first response was to crumple the note and toss it in the trash. Then I wanted to justify my behavior by making all the excuses that I listed earlier. Finally, I chided myself for not being a good priest. Even though I respond to scores of calls and letters asking for help, I had failed this time. I had withheld kind speech.

I didn't answer the letter right away. I took time to *be aware* of my desire for self-justification and then I had to (yet again!) *accept* the fact that I was not perfect and to *befriend* all sides of myself. I needed to remind myself to be more vigilant when I answered the phone, so that any personal anxiety or stress would not creep into the conversation (*a firm purpose of amendment*). When I was ready, I sent L. a simple note expressing my regret (*remorse*) at my behavior and offering prayers (*atonement*) for her friend.

This simple incident was the catalyst for a deeper learning experience. Workshop participants tell me that I'm compassionate and wise and it's all too easy to believe them and to allow my mindfulness to flag. Our resolve to mend our ways can become stagnant.

The road to transformation is like a spiral; we need to relearn everything, many times, and on deeper levels.

L. reminded me of this and I am grateful for her letter.

Transformation

Asking to be forgiven for our past actions is a good way to begin the process of transformation. We have already taken the first steps by becoming aware of the harm we have done, accepting responsibility for our actions, and then becoming intimate with the dark side of our nature that causes harm. We have even felt remorse and made amends. That may take care of the past, but now it's time to look to the present and future. Unfortunately, just because we regret something hurtful that we've done doesn't mean that we'll never repeat the action. Keep the awareness of harmful actions sharp by trying this:

❀ Practice: Daily Inventory ❀

In the evening, before you go to sleep, sit quietly and reflect on your day. Begin with the morning and trace your daily activities. Recall any hurtful thoughts, words, or actions that you performed. If it's helpful, write them down. Be as thorough and honest as you can. Remember any unkind thoughts you had about your family or co-workers. Recall impatient words directed at fellow commuters, co-workers, and telephone solicitors. Consider harmful actions, from the gravest to the seemingly trivial: elbowing aside someone on the train, taking a box of paper clips from the office, tossing a candy wrapper out the car window.

If it's appropriate, resolve to apologize to anyone you've harmed. If it's not feasible, then close your eyes, take several deep breaths, being aware of your chest or abdomen rising and falling, and then silently say the forgiveness phrase:

> *For all the harm I have done to you, knowingly or unknowingly, forgive me.*
> *I wish you well.*

Then resolve to be more mindful the next day. If you have

written down your transgressions, then crumple the paper and throw it away. You have repented; let go of any residual guilt.

Do this exercise daily, weekly, or whenever you feel the need.

Transformation doesn't happen overnight. It is a slow process of honing our awareness of our actions. During a self-help meeting, a woman raised her hand to speak. She was elated to tell the following story. The previous day, she had purchased a sweater and the clerk had undercharged her. As she was leaving the store, Ann counted her change and realized the mistake. She returned to the shop and gave back the money. This may seem like normal behavior, but to Ann it was a monumental step forward. In the past, she had always bargained hard and had even switched tags on items to get a lower price. Sometimes she bought one scarf and stuffed a stolen one in her bag. This time, she had automatically done the right thing. Awareness had paid off.

We keep vigilant because any harm we do another harms us as well. Here are the words of the Buddha:

> *Our life is shaped by our mind; we become what we think.*
>   *Suffering follows an evil thought as the wheels of a cart*
>   *follow the oxen that draw it.*
> *Our life is shaped by our mind; we become what we think. Joy*
>   *follows a pure thought like a shadow that never leaves.*

So after atoning for what we have done, we can begin to cultivate an attitude of kindness and generosity.

❋ Practice: Greet the Day with Gratitude ❋

When you awaken each morning, greet the day with a prayer, thought, or phrase expressing gratitude. This mind-state can set a positive tone for the day. We can become so enmeshed in our problems, both great and small, that we forget that we have been given the gift of life. We share that gift with millions of beings that all want the same things: safety, happiness, health, and strength. Reflect that we are all children in the same family. Don't exclude anyone.

May all beings be happy and live together in harmony.

The wonderful thing about having free will is that we are never pre-ordained to act in a certain way. We always have a choice. Even if we have become aware that we have a propensity to lie or steal, it doesn't mean that we have to act out our tendency. We can be creative and counteract. If you are prone to harsh words, make an effort to use kind speech. I know that often I might admire someone's new dress, but I may not comment on it. Why not? It doesn't cost me anything. If you are tempted to cheat or penny-pinch, make overt acts of generosity. If you spend your free time amusing yourself, then decide to volunteer once a week helping others.

Cultivating a joyful mind benefits all beings. When we experience joy, the positive energy radiates from every pore. It's like being a fairy godmother with a magic wand. Everyone we touch is infected with well-being, and that well-being spreads throughout the community. When there is joy there is no room for harmful thoughts, words, or actions.

❧ 3 ❧

Forgiving Others

For all the harm others have done to me,
knowingly or unknowingly, I forgive you.

Some of us find it difficult to forgive. Each slight and harsh word is seen as an attack on our personhood. Every time someone bumps into us on the street or overcharges us, the assault enters our memory bank. When we are fired from a job, or divorced, the hurt and anger can make us physically ill. Even when the resentment fades away, a tinge of bitterness remains that colors the way we view ourselves and the world. We either live life as a contest—me against everyone else—or see ourselves as victims. When we allow what happens to us to define who we are, then we give up our freedom to evolve and grow. Feelings of powerlessness or thoughts of revenge make us rigid and imprison us as surely as the defenses we build to avoid being hurt further.

But who are we protecting? Before we can
think about forgiving the harm others have
done us and letting go of resentment, we first
have to find out who has been harmed.

🌸 Practice: Who Am I? 🌸

Imagine that you are at a gathering where you don't recognize anyone. A stranger approaches you and introduces himself. Then it's your turn. Who are you?

Get paper and pencil and jot down as quickly as possible the things that come into your mind when you are asked who you are. Just take a couple of minutes and when nothing further pops up, stop writing.

You may have written your name, but Shakespeare wrote, "A rose by any other name would smell as sweet." I know several people who have changed their first names for aesthetic reasons, and nowadays there are so many marriages and divorces that last names change yearly. Your schoolmates may give you a nickname and your sweetheart calls you "Honey." When I was baptized, I was called Madeline Ann; when I was confirmed, I took the name Therese. Many years later, I became a Buddhist and was dubbed Shoshin, and when I took priestly vows, I was called Ko-i. I have many names; is any one of them really me? So, if we are not our names, who are we?

You probably listed your profession. I am a doctor, a designer, a teacher, a student. But we can be laid off from work, change careers in midlife, graduate from university. Twenty years ago, when I sold my graphic design business and moved to East Hampton, I felt lost. I was no longer president of a corporation (albeit a small one). I no longer had a brownstone apartment in Manhattan with a sports car in the garage. I had no place to wear the beautiful clothes I had accumulated. When people asked me about myself, I struggled to find an answer and talked about things I used to do. What about now? Did I cease to exist because I didn't have a career? It happens to all of us at some time or other—we lose a job or retire and begin to wonder: "Who am I?"

You may have mentioned your relationships: spouse, parent, partner. But there can be divorce or death; children grow up and leave the nest; your partner finds his next true love. Do you cease to exist because a relationship ends?

We may collect things—stylish clothes, a better car, a bigger house, a more exotic garden, hoping that our possessions will shore up our sense of self. Eventually, we realize that we are not our possessions. All of the "stuff" that we accrue is ephemeral. Everything is bound to get old, lost, or forgotten. Our attachment to things fades and we see that nothing lasts forever.

We are not our bodies. Sometimes we are struck by illness and our bodies let us down. The despair I experienced when I contracted Lyme's disease warped my whole outlook—I could no longer run marathons or triathlons, and a residue of arthritis left me unable to windsurf. As my physical capabilities dwindled, so did my confidence in myself.

How much more difficult it is when cancer or AIDS or ALS sneaks up to infiltrate a healthy body? When a surgeon removes a breast, or our hair falls out because of chemotherapy, or we're crippled with arthritis, we may ask, "Who am I?" and come to realize that we are not our bodies.

So who are you?

Here is a Zen koan:

When you remove the wheels and axle from a cart, what's left?

When you remove your name, your role, your possessions, your beliefs, your body, what's left?

❦ Practice: Who Are You? ❦

Sit in a comfortable meditation posture and compose yourself by watching your breath. It may help your concentration to count your exhalations from one through ten. When you reach ten, begin again at one. If your mind wanders, or you're distracted by sounds, begin at number one.

After a while, the numbers will fall away, but you'll still be aware of your breath. At this time, silently ask yourself, "Who am I?" When ideas or insights arise, simply return to your breath and ask, "Who am I?"

You can continue the simple practice of asking "Who am I?" during meditation or while taking long walks, weeding the garden, or vacuuming the rug.

You may discover that your perception of yourself changes depending on time, place, relationship, or how others perceive you and how you perceive others. You may discover that the solid, separate self you cling to is a chimera. There is nothing permanent that you can point to as being "you." The idea of "you" is like an ice cube, seemingly solid, but when you try to hold it in your hand, it melts into water and slips through your fingers. The drops that trickle to the ground disappear, dried by the sun.

> *If you are not your name, your career,*
> *your relationships, your possessions or*
> *your body, then who is being harmed?*

You might have to continue the search for a long time to find your true self, but it's the exploration that's important. We all trudge through life carrying backpacks filled with pre-conceptions and judgments. But each time we are able to discard just one preconception, it is like removing a stone from the pack, and our steps become lighter, our vision, clearer. The journey becomes a joyful adventure.

As we taste this freedom, we begin to realize that there is nobody to be harmed. As the quest continues, we awaken to the truth that there is also nobody harming us.

Forgiving the Small Stuff

Our natural, human inclination is to cling to anything that's pleasant. Unfortunately, the habit becomes so ingrained that we also hold on to things that are not only unpleasant, but downright unwholesome and dangerous to our well-being. We attach ourselves like remoras to a shark, suctioning its blood. Although the remora can live on its own, the more it depends on the shark for food, the more it loses its ability to fend for itself. When someone harms us, we tend to cling to the incident and feed on its negativity. The negative energy infuses our minds and hearts until all of our thoughts and actions are tainted. We are no longer free to act from a clear place of awareness. We are trapped by something that happened in the past and although it is painful, we doggedly hold on to resentments until we are prisoners of the past.

It's not easy to forgive. Before we can move on to major transgressions, we must train ourselves by letting go of the little things. It's like lifting weights—start with five pounds before you move up to 25 pounds.

But before you pick up that first weight, ask yourself how you respond to harm.

Reacting

Sometimes it's the physical body that's hurt, but usually it is the idea of our self that is damaged. Someone has attacked our carefully constructed persona. For many of us, the easiest way to deal with our hurt is to counterattack. So the cycle of harm continues. But there is another way.

❧ Practice: Breaking the Cycle of Harm ❧

When a person verbally assaults you, take a couple of deep breaths. Then silently send the person loving-kindness, by repeating the phrases:

May you be happy and peaceful.
I wish you well.

This may seem wimpy and passive, but it is active in a creative way. Martial artists engage the opponent's forward, attacking energy instead of expending more of their own. When negative energy is directed toward us, we can actually transform that energy into a positive force. Loving-kindness is the catalyst. We are not turning the other cheek, asking for more abuse; we are extending our hands in a gesture of understanding. No matter whether the cutting words are deliberate or thoughtless, we simply acknowledge that we all share the same desire to be happy.

The other person doesn't need to know what you are doing; it is enough that you know. It is a form of forgiveness.

Once, when I was in one of my super-efficient modes, planning a retreat, I hurt someone's feelings without even suspecting it. I was surprised to learn that the person was upset and only realized what I had done when she told me that she had been sending me loving-kindness every day since the incident. I felt humbled and resolved not to act that way again, although I've slipped hundreds of times.

Since that time, when I'm about to be embroiled in an argument, I've tried to take a few deep breaths and repeat the loving-kindness phrases. It gives me time to compose myself, and my non-reaction defuses the situation.

This takes lots of mindfulness because most of us are pro-grammed to react, but it's possible to bring ourselves back to the present moment. All it takes is a couple of mindful breaths. Why is it important to be in the present moment? The harm is occurring now, isn't it?

Not always. The unkind action usually triggers the sub-conscious memory of some previous hurt. Whether we are wounded or not depends on our state of well-being in the present moment.

When something annoying or painful happens, I tend to overreact. Near the beginning of my meditation studies, my teacher sent me on a month-long retreat. I was nowhere near ready to undertake such a task, but I went anyway.

The retreat took place in a converted factory in a decay-ing city; not exactly the bucolic, serene setting I had envi-sioned. I felt overwhelmed by the long hours sitting in medi-tation posture, the brutal heat and humidity, and the constant noise and toxic odors that emanated from the paint factory across the street. The students at the center were busy with work projects and I seldom had a meeting with the teacher. I felt overworked and overlooked—there were two people who were "head trainees," and me. They practiced leading liturgy and preparing the altar, while I got up before dawn to make coffee, sound the wake-up bells, and time all the meditation sessions. During work practice, they did research and wrote reports, while I scrubbed kitchen walls, cleaned out vacant lots, and did laundry. One weekend, while I slept alone on the floor of the meditation hall, there was a break-in. Luckily, I used earplugs to stay asleep and did not hear the prowlers, and they did not notice me sleeping behind the altar. Afterward, I felt I had been in great danger, but the leaders of the center focused on what had been stolen, not on my safety.

Several days later, during the evening meditation period I noticed a large roach skittering across the floor. A monk raised his arm to smash it, but one of the head trainees said, "Oh no, don't kill it." I sat in my seat and fumed. After I rang the bell that ended the period, I stood up and shouted, "I have to sleep here, you don't! Kill it or get rid of it!" The head trainee replied that it was a living creature just like us and shouldn't be killed. By then the roach had disappeared into one of the many hiding places in the vast room.

My anger at the trainee and fear that the roach would crawl over me kept me awake through the night as I gnashed my teeth and tossed and turned. Who were these people to decide that a roach was more important than I was? If this was enlightenment, I didn't want it. The next morning I packed up and left. It was only three days before the retreat was to end.

I held on to my righteous anger and resentment for a long time. It took months of sitting meditation before I realized that the roach was simply the final straw. The people at the center were not meeting my need to be special, to be important, to be recognized, and that tapped into a buried suspicion that I was just not good enough. No one had been ganging up on me; people were just going about their business. The sinister plot against me existed only in my imagination and it was fed by my subconscious fear of being nobody.

Now I am happy during those fleeting moments when "I" become nobody; when the ice melts.

When we are not attached to a fixed image of ourselves, then we can drop our prickly defenses and our stance of "I am right and you are wrong." Only then we can forgive.

A few months later, I attended a retreat at a different center. The rustic building was situated on a large tract of fields and woods, and the people seemed welcoming and friendly. I had a peaceful retreat and felt happy and connected. When I returned home, my truck was not in the driveway. I had lent it to an employee. Later, she arrived and told me she had crashed into a tree and the truck was badly damaged. I asked if she were hurt and then went on about the business of calling the insurance company. There was no anger or regret. I just did what had to be done and didn't view this mishap as a diabolic scheme devised by the universe to unsettle me.

Why did I react differently to the two situations? In the first instance, I was constricted by the old story of who I was and how I should be treated. In the second, I approached the situation with a fresh outlook, with no preconceptions of how things were supposed to be, and I acted in the present moment.

✸ Practice: Staying in the Present ✸

The more often we can live in the present, the easier our lives and relationships will be. It's no accident that most meditation practices focus on being aware of what is going on now. Whenever you feel overcome by painful memories of the past or nervousness about the future, try this:

Sit comfortably in a quiet place and begin by watching your breath rise and fall. Each time you inhale, you can silently note "in" and as you exhale, note "out." Don't just spit out the words mechanically, but try to draw them out to the same length as your inhalation or exhalation. Innnn; Ouuuut. After a time, you may notice that there is a brief space between one exhalation and the next inhalation, so that the cycle becomes: in—out—space. As you relax, you may notice a rhythm inherent in the breath—it may feel like floating on a gently rolling sea. When thoughts come into your mind, note "thinking" and return to your breath.

Connect to your breath as coming from your body. It may

help to place your hand on your chest or abdomen to feel it rising and falling.

After a time you can open to sounds around you, letting them go in one ear and out the other.

When you get lost in thought, come back to your breath.

When you are just breathing, just listening, then you are in the present moment.

Withdrawing

Another way we respond to harsh words or actions is to withdraw. We don't express anger and it is buried inside to fester into resentment and depression. We refuse to acknowledge our true feelings. We may not even know what we feel; we put our heads in the sand, avoiding the obvious. At times like these, it is helpful to identify what you are feeling at the moment you were hurt.

❁ Practice: Befriending Your Feelings ❁

During this exercise, we become aware of our feelings and then become intimate with them. Emotions are not ignored and buried deep inside, but are taken out and aired, like laundry hung on a line in the fresh air. Each breath of awareness clears our hearts of the need to store up moldy resentments.

1. Take pencil and paper and write down all the feelings that occurred during the incident. Here are some examples:

anger	indignity	vengeance	depression
irritation	frustration	worthlessness	annoyance
persecution	isolation	embarrassment	hostility
rejection	fear	vulnerability	confusion
betrayal	hurt	apprehension	insecurity
sadness	helplessness	diminishment	nervousness
outrage	rage	despair	resentment

If you have written down several words, work with one feeling at a time.

2. Close your eyes and take a couple of deep, cleansing breaths, and then watch your breath as you did in the previous meditation. When you are ready, name the emotion you are feeling and claim it as your own, saying, for example, "I feel betrayed."

3. Try to notice where the emotion resides in your body. Emotions frequently manifest as rigidity in the neck and shoulders, a roiling stomach, or tightness in the chest or heart area. Focus on that area of the body where you feel contraction or tension. If you cannot identify a spot, then do a brief body scan, starting at the top of your head, moving through your face, neck, shoulders, arms, torso, and legs until you find a tense area.

4. Let go of all thoughts that relate to why you feel the emotion and place your full attention on being intimate with the sensation.

5. Then, begin to notice the quality of the sensation. Is it pleasant or unpleasant? Is it tingling or prickling or throbbing? Is it sharp or dull? Is it obvious or subtle?

After you have investigated the feeling for a while, notice if it becomes stronger or weaker. Does it stay in the same place or migrate to another part of the body? Is it still there at all?

6. When you have worked with the difficult emotions you wrote down and they seem to have dissipated, then begin to identify what you are feeling right now.

Write down what you are feeling now. Here are some suggestions:

relieved	light	peaceful	tranquil
happy	disappointed	elated	serene
grateful	relaxed	satisfied	uneasy
calm	dissatisfied	contented	comfortable
pleased	composed		

7.   Then repeat steps 2 through 5, meditating on becoming intimate with the emotion, its quality and presence in your being.

When we befriend our feelings, then we become free
to face the person who harmed us without rancor.

One of the best things about mindfulness is that it brings us into balance. If we tend to counterattack when someone hurts us, then a moment of mindfulness gives us time to act thoughtfully and compassionately. If we tend to hold in our hurt and anger, then awareness lets us know exactly how we feel and gives us courage to express those feelings to the other person. It isn't necessary to hold everything inside. It's important to let the other person know that they harmed you. Sometimes the harm is unintentional, caused by the other person's lack of mindfulness.

The forgiveness phrase is: For all the harm you have done me, knowingly or unknowingly, I forgive you. Just because someone acted unintentionally doesn't mean that he can't learn and grow. If you don't gently call him on his transgressions, then the thoughtless actions will continue. When we find the delicate balance between aggressive response and wimping out, then we can act without an agenda. We say what we feel without expecting anything in return. We simply clear the air (and by the way, our own heart and mind).

When someone asks you for forgiveness, what is your first reaction? If it's "Not in this lifetime!" then it's time to go back to basics. Take a few deep breaths and tell the person that you have to think about it. Then go back and redo the "Befriending Your Feelings" practice on page 45. Sometimes a person who seeks forgiveness truly regrets what she has done; other times the words "I'm sorry, forgive me," seem like the easiest way to avoid conflict. Don't worry about her motives; just look into your own heart to discover what is best for your state of mind. Saying "I forgive you" may make the other person feel better, but if the resentment is still cluttering up your mind and heart, it doesn't do much for you.

Many times a person is oblivious to the hurt he has caused and doesn't ask for forgiveness, but that doesn't mean that you can't forgive him anyway. We are only responsible for our own behavior.

Our practice of forgiveness continues every day. Each time you think you have been wronged, try to remember to take a couple of deep breaths and send loving-kindness to your antagonist. If, after the incident, you still feel unsettled, then do the exercise to discover and befriend your feelings. As your "muscles" get stronger then you can attempt the next level.

Forgiving the Big Stuff

The more we forgive, the more we cultivate an atmosphere of openness and receptivity. We begin by acknowledging and accepting our own feelings and, little by little, we come to accept other people's idiosyncrasies. Words and actions that once raised our hackles now raise a smile of understanding instead. This newfound equanimity is tested when someone does us graver harm.

What if your home is broken into and all your valuables are stolen?

Here's what a Zen monk wrote two centuries ago:
The moon at my window.
The thief, he left it there.
—Ryokan

Ryokan was penniless and lived in a secluded hut in the forest. His only possessions were his robe, his begging bowl, and the cushion he used for meditation. When he returned and found his meager belongings gone, he responded not with outrage but with understanding. One can interpret his poem as wistful irony—the thief took everything else, why did he forget the moon?

On the other hand, the moon belongs to everyone, and so do all things. Who can say that anything is really ours alone? Native Americans have an adage: "A bowl belongs to whomever needs it." Latinos may say, "Mi casa, su casa." A few years ago, when a valuable statue of Kuan Yin, the goddess of compassion, was stolen from a temple, the Zen priest responded that the thief might have needed the money it would bring. The statue was gone, but the compassion was not.

What is truly important, temporal things that get old, lost, and broken, or the eternal—the sun, moon, stars?

🏵 Practice: Releasing Attachments 🏵

Write down items that belong to you. Don't worry about listing them in order of importance; just jot them down as they come into your mind. Keep writing until you can't think of any more or there is no more space on the paper.

Sit quietly for a few minutes while focusing on your breath. When you're ready, look at the list and cross out one thing that you wouldn't miss if it were taken away. Keep crossing out the unimportant items. When you reach a point where you feel as if you cannot live without the item, stop. Put down the list and come back to it later and cross out another item. It may take several days, but you'll find that you'll be able to let go of most of the items. Therefore, if your things are damaged or stolen, you will survive.

Seeing that most possessions are not necessary, are you willing to forgive the vandal, thief, or natural disaster? Can you open to compassion to the perpetrator? Even accidental harm is difficult to forgive.

One morning a friend called me in tears. The day before, she had witnessed a terrible accident on the highway—two trucks collided in a fiery explosion a few feet in front of her own car. She was shaken, but grateful to have emerged unscathed. She continued on her round of chores, and on the way home, there was a detour because of the accident. As she traveled unfamiliar roads at dusk, a dog ran in front of her car and she hit it. She dissolved into tears and was profoundly shocked at having hurt an animal. The dog's owner ran over to her and embraced her, assuring her it was not her fault. The owner comforted my friend and then calmly went about lifting the dog into her car and taking it to the vet, where it was put down. How many of us can forgive that kind of hurt and then turn around and offer compassion to the person responsible for our loss?

What if someone harms us or our loved ones? I know a woman who was sexually molested and physically abused as a child. The taste of fear and repugnance lingered after many years, and she could not forgive. The memory of the degradation and pain is with her everyday. How can we ask her to forgive her abuser?

The phrase, "For all the harm you have done me, knowingly or unknowingly, I forgive you" can be adapted. Just add, "as much as I can."

For all the harm you have done me, knowingly or unknowingly, I forgive you as much as I can.

🌺 Practice: Beginning to Forgive—As Much as You Can 🌺

Center yourself by watching your breath. Then begin to send loving-kindness to yourself.

May I be safe from harm.
May I be happy and peaceful.
May I be strong and healthy.
May I live my life joyfully.

Form an image of yourself and regard it with tenderness. Gently repeat the phrases, always keeping contact with the image of yourself. It may help to say silently one of the phrases each time you exhale. When you begin to feel calm and relaxed, call to mind a picture of the person who harmed you and say the forgiveness phrase:

For all the harm you have done me, knowingly or
unknowingly, I forgive you as much as I can.
As I wish myself to be safe, happy and peaceful,
so I wish you well.
May you live your life with ease.

If you feel a tug of resistance when you say the phrase, then take a couple of deep breaths and return to sending the loving-kindness to yourself.

May I be safe from harm.
May I be happy and peaceful.
May I be strong and healthy.
May I live my life joyfully.

When your tension has eased you can say:

I am willing to forgive you, but not yet.

When you do this meditation, it's important to be compassionate to yourself. If the harm has left profound damage to body, mind, and spirit, it will be hard to forgive. But your intention is vital. Each drop of willingness to forgive erodes the resentment. Eventually, jagged rocks become smooth stones. Forgiveness is a process and occurs in its own time.

Forgive yourself for not being able to forgive.

I am willing to forgive, but not yet.

Forgiving the Unforgivable

After the Columbine massacre, members of a local church planted 15 linden trees as a memorial to the 15 people who had been killed—the 13 victims and two shooters. A couple of weeks later, while onlookers cheered, some parents of the dead children marked 13 trees with the names of the victims and chopped down the remaining two that represented the killers.

The depth of grief and the resulting anger can be understood because it was so fresh, but the following year, one of the victim's relatives destroyed two of the 15 crosses that had been erected as tribute to the slain. Forgiveness had not yet blossomed.

Each of us reacts differently when we experience great harm or loss. During a camping trip, a seven-year-old girl was abducted from her family. Her mother, Marietta, was filled with fear and a desire for revenge, but she made a decision to change her attitude to one of forgiveness. She began to think positive thoughts about the kidnapper and eventually, when a suspect was apprehended, Marietta met with him and her compassionate presence led him to confess to killing her daughter and three other children. When he was taken to his cell he hanged himself. Marietta reached out to his mother, for each had lost a child. Together they visit their children's graves each year and Marietta now lectures to families of victims of violence on forgiveness and reconciliation.

Marietta has set us an example in letting go of the need for revenge and in transforming negative energy into positive healing. When you are irreparably damaged by someone and are locked in feelings of bitterness, try this:

❧ Practice: Transforming Negative Energy ❧

Begin by centering yourself in whatever way is most comfortable for you. When you feel ready, imagine that the bitterness, outrage, or any other negative emotion that you feel manifests in front of you as a miasma of hot, heavy, dark smoke. Each time you inhale, try to experience the taste, smell, texture of the smoke. Be willing to take it into yourself and when you exhale, transform it into light, bright, cool healing.

It may be helpful to inhale through your nose and exhale through your mouth, but if you experience resistance to taking in the smoke, then downgrade it to a dark cloud or fog. Don't think about what caused the negative emotion or who caused you harm. Just continue to breathe in hot, heavy, dark and breathe out light, bright, cool.

If you are willing, call to mind all the people who are feeling the same way you feel; people who have experienced the same hurt or loss that you have felt. Take in their emotion along with your own and send out light, bright, cool healing.

After some time, imagine that all the people who have received positive energy from you are so grateful that they return the energy one hundred-fold. So breathe in the light, bright, cool energy and bask in the glow of love and healing.

This meditation helps us on several levels. First, we acknowledge that we harbor negative feelings. Instead of ignoring them, we become willing to take them into our inner being and accept them. Remember that our usual mode is to react or withdraw. In this meditation, we call up the courage to respond in a different manner. We put the focus on ourselves and our feelings instead of the outside forces that have hurt us. We are creating a buffer zone that keeps us from acting out in a damaging way to the perpetrator, or retreating into fantasies of revenge. The actor/writer Malachy McCourt said, "Resentment is like taking poison and waiting for the other person to die."

We take responsibility for handling our feelings and move on to the next step of transforming the energy. We have been victimized once by the harm-doer;

We don't have to victimize ourselves by being held in thrall to our emotions.

How empowering that is!

When we have been the objects of harm, we isolate ourselves. We tend to curl up into a little ball of self-pity and separate ourselves from others. No one has been hurt like I have, we think. This meditation helps us recognize that there are many people who are suffering as we suffer. We reach out to them and take in their feelings and send out healing to them. We reunite with the human race.

We are not depleting our energy, because it returns to us a hundred-fold.

Transforming the negative energy within ourselves paves

the way to forgive our victimizer. It may be helpful to reflect that your tormentor is a human being just like yourself. He or she began his or her life wanting the same things you want—love, acceptance, and happiness.

❧ Practice: Recalling Our Common Human Essence ❧

Sit quietly and begin to send loving-kindness to yourself, using the phrases that are most meaningful to you. After a time, call to mind the person who has harmed you. Visualize the person as a toddler or a baby, sleeping quietly in a crib or in his or her mother's arms and begin to send the person loving-kindness.

> *For all the harm you have done me, knowingly or*
> *   unknowingly, I forgive you as much as I can.*
> *As I wish myself to be happy, so I wish you to be happy.*
> *As I wish to my heart to be filled with peace, so I wish*
> *   your heart be filled with peace.*
> *I wish you well.*

Imagine the sleeping child dreaming of the same things that all human beings desire: safety, happiness, peace, and love. If strong resistance arises, simply say, "I am willing to forgive you, but not yet."

Then send yourself compassion:

> *May I be free from pain.*
> *May I be free from suffering.*
> *May my heart be filled with peace.*

It doesn't matter if you don't yet mean the sentiments expressed in the meditation. You are cultivating willingness by "acting as if." You are dismantling the wall of resistance chink by chink. It may take some time, but eventually the light of forgiveness will shine forth. In the meantime, be considerate of yourself.

Some grave harm has not been committed to us personally, but is so horrible that its legacy haunts several generations. The Holocaust, the bombing of Hiroshima, slavery—the list is endless. How can we forgive such atrocities?

I read a story in a newsmagazine about two Benedictine nuns in Rwanda. During the massacre of the Tutsi minority by the Hutus, thousands of Tutsis requested asylum in the nuns' compound. The nuns, who were Hutus, went to the militia asking that the convent be "cleared." The militia killed more than 7,000 Tutsis. Most were hacked to death with machetes; others were burned alive in a garage. One of the nuns provided gasoline for the fire. During their trial for war crimes, the nuns asked for understanding and acquittal, saying that they would have been killed if the refugees had not been turned in.

How could women who had dedicated their lives to God and service to human beings betray their faith? Was it terror, hatred, or living in an atmosphere of death and destruction?

Here is St. Francis of Assisi's prayer:

Lord, make me a channel of thy peace,
That where there is hatred, I may bring love;
That where there is wrong, I may bring the spirit
*   of forgiveness;*
That where there is discord, I may bring harmony;
That where there is error, I may bring truth;
That where there is doubt, I may bring faith;
That where there is despair, I may bring hope;
That where there are shadows, I may bring light;
That where there is sadness, I may bring joy.

Lord grant that I may seek rather to comfort,
*   than be comforted;*

To understand, than to be understood;
To love, than be loved.
For it is in self-forgetting that one finds.
It is by forgiving that one is forgiven.
It is by dying that one awakens to Eternal Life.

We can only bring light when we have fully experienced shadow. How can we understand joy until we have delved into our own sadness? If we are honest with ourselves, we will see that, depending on the circumstances, we are all equally capable of despicable behavior and heroic, compassionate acts. Like the yin/yang symbol, the seeds of good and evil nestle side by side in our hearts.

✳ Practice: Cultivating Compassion for Those Who Cause Harm ✳

Let's reflect on some of the opposite qualities in the prayer. First write down any instances when you:

caused discord	were sad	needed comfort
were in shadow	were doubtful	felt despair
made an error		

Then, remember those times when you:

created harmony	were joyful	engendered hope
basked in light	lived in faith	brought comfort
were truthful		

Now write down any scenario in which you could imagine yourself:
- killing
- betraying
- stealing
- lying
- cheating

If you came up with nothing, ask yourself these questions:

If my father were dying in agony of an incurable disease, would I help him commit suicide?

If it were a choice of saving my family or betraying a neighbor, what would I do?

If my child were starving to death, would I steal bread?

If I needed a job, would I lie about my education on the application?

If I could get away with it, would I cheat on my income tax?

If my combat unit committed crimes against humanity, would I go along, report the acts, desert?

It's not as cut and dried as we think. With this practice, we begin to understand that all humans share the same qualities and we can never predict how we will react in dire circumstances. Fear, anger, hatred are like crouching tigers in our hearts, waiting to pounce. It is by forgiving that one is forgiven. When we forgive another, then we also forgive ourselves.

Accepting an Apology

When someone shows remorse and asks for forgiveness, we can grant it or not. It's our choice. If we are not ready, then we can truthfully say that it is too soon for us and we'll consider it after more time has passed. (I am willing to forgive you, but not yet.) However,

When we do agree to forgive, then we owe it to ourselves to do it wholeheartedly, putting aside blame.

It's enough to say, "I forgive you." Rehashing the details of the incident and how badly you felt, and how it disrupted your life is not at all helpful. Putting the person on the defensive curdles genuine remorse and may even give rise to additional harm.

Forgetting

An old song says, "It's easy to remember and so hard to forget." Even if we forgive a wrong, the memory of the hurt remains and affects how we respond to the events of our lives. If we have been betrayed once, it takes a while to trust again. If we have been abandoned, we lack a sense of security. If we have been brutalized, we may shrink from affection.

> *The only way to cope with the vestiges of harmis to acknowledge and honor them.*

Forgetting is a gradual process and one day you'll realize that any residual resentment is gone and you'll be able to greet new situations without withdrawing. My friend Ann was abandoned by her fiancée. It was only a few weeks before the wedding and he decided he loved someone else. She was devastated and for several years the memory of the betrayal eroded her trust in men. Ann avoided close relationships because she feared that there was something wrong with herself; that she was unlovable. She feared that she would be disappointed again. Exploring her feelings of worthlessness and distrust helped. Here's how to do it.

❋ Practice: Honoring Feelings ❋

Sit in your normal meditation posture and begin to watch your breath. When you are settled, name the emotion that still haunts you.

Try to locate where in the body it resides and explore the

sensation as we've done before, noticing its texture: Is it smooth or rough; slimy or scratchy; silky or fuzzy?

Examine its temperature: Is it freezing or burning; hot or cold; cool or warm?

Observe its sound: Is it growling or purring; screeching or chirping; clashing or melodic; loud or soft?

Taste it: Is it bitter or sweet; peppery or salty; lumpy or smooth?

Smell it: Is it acrid or flowery; putrid or fresh; pungent or neutral?

What color is it? Examine the color: Is it vivid or pastel; muddy or clear; dark or faded?

As you carefully observe the qualities of the emotion, do you notice any change?

When you pay attention to the emotion, it will fade. Each time the residue of harm sneaks up and curtails your freedom, sit down and confront it. Like a ghost, it will fade into the mist.

Another way to acknowledge that harm has been done is to bear witness to the event. To remember the anniversary of the bombing of Hiroshima, a Zen center in California has created a tradition to bear witness to the harm caused on that day. On the afternoon preceding the anniversary, the residents climb to the top of the local mountain. It's not a treacherous climb, but it is tricky, especially for people who are elderly or not in good physical condition. It can take from two to four hours, and when the summit is reached, there is only a rocky, uneven plateau to camp on. At night, if the sky is clear, millions of stars are visible. The next morning before dawn, a bell awakens everyone and a sunrise memorial service is held. It is a way of honoring the victims who died or were maimed, but also reminds us to bear witness to the harm we have done. Even though we may not even have been born when the bomb was dropped, we still share responsibility for the actions of our nation. In some indefinable way, the harm done has distorted our character. In recalling what was done, we atone—become at-one with our transgressions.

"Forgive and forget" sounds good, but sometimes we need to be reminded of the horrors that we are capable of committing. There is a Holocaust museum in Washington that graphically depicts our brutality to one another. The phrase, "Never again" is sometimes used to justify violence, but can also be used as a vow: I, as a member of the human community, vow never to brutalize my fellow creatures. By making this vow, we do not separate ourselves from the "evil-doers"; we recognize that because we are humans, we share responsibility for past actions and future ones. None of us acts alone.

More Unspeakable Acts

I had just finished writing the section "Forgiving the Unforgivable," when I took a break. It was ten o'clock in the morning and I made my first phone call of the day. The receptionist who answered the phone told me to turn on the television. I somewhat testily told her that I never watched morning TV, but she insisted that I turn it on. It was September 11 and I saw the twin towers of the World Trade Center collapse. During the rest of the day, I was riveted by the news, watching as one disaster followed another. I felt shocked and was filled with sadness. For the next few days, I woke up way before my normal time. There was a gnawing in my stomach and my jaw was so stiff that my teeth hurt. It was an opportunity to practice what I preach; to go beyond "why" I suffered, and explore the sensations themselves. Each time the churning in my stomach resumed, I placed my entire attention on it. It still returned, but it occurred less frequently, lasted for a shorter period of time, and was fainter.

While I was reorganizing the stacks of papers on my desk, I picked up a notebook that I carry to conferences. On the first page I had jotted down this quote by C. S. Lewis: "Whoever would have thought grief felt so much like fear . . ."

His words point to the truth of what we've been practicing: most negative emotions feel the same and sometimes we have trouble recognizing exactly what we feel. Although the terrorist attacks aroused feelings of loss and sadness, they also caused us to be fearful.

People responded differently to the tragedy. I have an acquaintance who lives in Manhattan who couldn't leave his building. He holed up, cocooned in his apartment, basking in a false sense of safety, withdrawing from what was happening around the corner. Some of us reacted by blaming the perpetrators, vowing vengeance, even harassing innocent Muslims and other Americans who happened to have emigrated from Eastern countries.

Others found the balance between the two extremes and transformed their difficult emotions into healing energy: praying, donating blood and food, joining rescue efforts, creating a community of caring—transformation in action.

In the weeks following the disaster, reactions became more diverse. Some people spoke of the cowardliness of the hijackers and the bravery of rescue workers. There were memorial services for people who died during the disaster, but scarcely a mention of the terrorists who died. They are fellow human beings. Do they deserve our prayers and forgiveness? If you cannot find it in your heart, you can simply express your willingness to relent: "I am willing to forgive you, but not yet."

When we feel that we cannot forgive, it is imperative
to ask ourselves again, "Who is being harmed?"
and return to the truth of interbeing.

I am you and you are me. There is no separation between us. Each of us harbors the potential for good and evil in our hearts. There is no them, there is only us. That's what forgiveness is about.

❦ 4 ❦

Forgiving Yourself

For all the harm I have done myself,
knowingly or unknowingly, I forgive myself.

When we think about forgiving ourselves, we generally mean forgiving transgressions we have committed against others. The victim may forgive us, God may forgive us, but often we don't forgive ourselves. We meander through a maze of could have, should have, would have. We are trapped in cul-de-sacs of guilt and shame.

After graduating from Marymount College in 1962, I went directly into the Peace Corps. It was an exciting time—a youngish John F. Kennedy had been newly installed as President and hopes were high that we could "do something for our country." The Peace Corps was brand-new and the siren song of adventure, travel to distant lands, and doing good was hard to resist. There was also a sense of being important, doing important deeds; an irresistible lure for wet-behind-the-ears college grads.

I would be sent to Ethiopia, and when the telegram announcing my selection arrived, I had to run to the atlas, for although I knew it was in Africa, I didn't know precisely where. We volunteers would train at Georgetown University for two months and then go on to Africa. What an adventure! In 1962 only the very rich, news correspondents, and explorers traveled to such exotic locales.

Several Ethiopian exchange students were hired to teach us the language, Amharic, and I fell in love with one of them. Unfortunately, having spent sixteen years in Catholic schools had not prepared me for this momentous occasion. At Marymount, we had been forced to attend classes like "hostess problems" to learn how to make tiny, crustless sandwiches, how to pour tea, and how to enter and exit a limousine gracefully. Sex education was a taboo subject, for good girls just didn't do it.

Before departing for Ethiopia, we recruits were prepared for anything, having received numerous inoculations for an alphabet soup of mysterious diseases. Teeth were inspected and Georgetown dental students drilled and filled every potential cavity. I learned to run a mile and climb a rope (not many Marymount girls in 1962 could do this—*so* unladylike!). I was taught to build a fire, dig a latrine, and even watched a film "How to Deliver a Baby." I was given a snakebite kit, malaria pills, and iodine tablets to purify water. One thing was neglected.

Although male volunteers were subjected to films showing the ravages of sexually transmitted disease, the women received no sex education. There was a brief mention that if we wanted "protection" we could make an appointment with the doctor. But I was a Marymount girl, and too embarrassed to ask for a diaphragm.

After several months in Ethiopia, my luck ran out and I became pregnant. Being ignorant, I didn't realize it at first, and when I did, I was frightened. Not only were single mothers pariahs in the early '60s, but I believed I would be letting down the entire USA. How could I tell my fellow volunteers, the group leader, and my parents? I traveled to the capital city and my boyfriend searched in vain for a doctor to perform an abortion. There was no way out, and I returned to my village, reconciled to having the child. My plan was to hide the pregnancy as long as possible, then fess up and be shipped home to face my family. As long as I was going to have the baby, I wanted to make sure that it was healthy and visited a Romanian obstetrician stationed at the local hospital to find out what to do. He said that he could abort the baby and the next day I found myself splayed on a wooden table in a mud hut on the doctor's property. The doctor was assisted by his wife. There was no anesthesia, no sterile instruments, no rubber gloves. There was pain and shame. A male child was aborted.

A deep sense of guilt and loss mingled with the sense of relief that I was free to finish my stint and that no one would find out about my pregnancy. I could not forgive myself. When nearby monks at a leper colony invited our group to a retreat, I could not pray, and I certainly could not take communion. I judged myself and found myself unworthy of forgiveness. I did not go to confession because I did not have "a firm purpose of amendment." In my heart, I knew that if I had to do it over again, I would make the same decision. I would not forgive myself. After a few months, I poured out my story to one of the priests, telling him that I was not worthy of absolution. What hubris! He smiled and said that God would forgive me and absolved me.

My way of coping was to forget the incident. But every time I saw a newborn child the memory arose and I felt sick inside. God might have forgiven me, but I still couldn't forgive myself.

Now abortion is legal in this country and many women

have the right to choose. I support their decisions, for I made the same choice. Not only do I support them, I forgive them for harming another. But can they forgive themselves? Can I forgive myself?

It's been more than 35 years since the abortion. Lately, I've begun to feel the loss of the child who today would have been a man, and regret for the grandchildren I might have known. Finally, I'm ready to resurrect the memory. Sometimes when I sit in meditation, the sadness is overwhelming, but I stay with it and let the tears flow down my cheeks. I feel the tightness in my chest and the salty tears that touch my lips. I go into that dark place in my mind where the memory is buried and recall the hours on that table in the hut. I become "at one" with them as I bear witness to the suffering I caused myself and my son. And now, I know that at that time in my life I could not have done otherwise. So I've forgiven myself.

That doesn't mean that I've forgotten. Recently I was moved to perform a ceremony for the lost child. I simply placed a flower in front of the statue of Jizo (Buddhist protector of women, children, and travelers) and said, "Forgive me."

I no longer feel superior to mothers who toss their babies into dumpsters or parents who abuse their children, because I, too, have lived with suffocating fear and confusion and acted out of it. Somehow it is enriching to realize that I am the same as them; that each of us has the potential to cause suffering. There is no "them." It is all me. That is my unborn son's gift to me.

*How freeing to be able to embrace my dark side,
knowing that it is an integral part of being human!
That is forgiveness.*

Accepting Yourself

Loving-kindness is the foundation of forgiveness, but sometimes the most difficult person to love unconditionally is yourself. We hold ourselves to impossible standards of perfection, and when we fail to meet them, we feel worthless. Loving-kindness begins with ourselves.

❧ Practice: Honoring Your Self ❧

The purpose of this meditation is to open our hearts to love and acceptance for ourselves. Take several really deep breaths, being aware of your breath going in and out, feeling your chest or abdomen rise and fall. As you feel your breath rising and falling, visualize yourself as you are now, or at some other time in your life. Place yourself in a favorite setting—in your study, a garden, by the shore. Try to imagine as much detail as possible. See your clothes, your shoes and notice how your hair looks. Are you sitting, standing, or walking? When your image seems arranged comfortably, begin to say these phrases:

May I love myself exactly as I am.
May I be happy with things just as they are.

Just keep repeating the phrases.
Inhale, then as you exhale silently say:

May I love myself exactly as I am.

Inhale, then exhale and say:

May I be happy with things just as they are.

Continue with this rhythmic breathing and repetition of the phrases. If a voice whispers (or shouts) that you don't deserve love, that you are unworthy, then say:

For all the harm I have done to others, knowingly or
    unknowingly, I forgive myself.
For all the harm I have done myself, knowingly or

unknowingly, I forgive myself.

Then continue the loving-kindness meditation.

May I love myself exactly as I am.
May I be happy with things just as they are.

If there are other phrases that are more meaningful to you, feel free to use them. Some suggestions are:

May I love and accept myself.
May my heart and soul find peace.
May I find joy and happiness.

Harming Others

Sometimes we feel guilt and shame about some actions we have committed, and although the persons we harmed may have forgiven us, we have not forgiven ourselves. Each failure to act honorably gnaws at our already fragile self-esteem. During the meditation, memories of these transgressions may arise unbidden. It is time to face them and yourself. It is time to forgive yourself for being fully human.

When we have some detachment from the incident, it's possible to learn and grow. We discover that we are the same as everyone else, sharing the same failings. Because we are part of the whole, we also share the same virtues. We come back into balance, to our center, and if at a later time we have a choice to cause (or not cause) harm we don't automatically slide into harming behavior.

When I attended self-help meetings, I met Miracle Max. He was a tough-looking man who had been in prison for drug dealing and other felonies. The stories he told about his life as a dealer and user were hair-raising and sordid, but as the group listened, we felt a vicarious thrill, as well. It was like watching an episode of "Law & Order."

At first, I was a bit nervous around him, because he still carried an aura of potential danger, but as I learned how he had transformed his life, he became a model. He was a mentor to many young men who were trying to break their drug habits, and he returned to college to become a counselor. Max helped hundreds of youths. He had taken his worst flaw and, learning from it, had made it an asset. He counseled from his personal experience and was able to connect with people who were going through what he had gone through.

We all have the potential to learn from our
mistakes and transform our behavior.

The Five Families

In one Buddhist sect, each human being is thought to belong to a specific category or family. Certain major characteristics define each family and each is given a color. As we begin to truly know and accept ourselves, it may be helpful to explore each family. Although we all have some of the traits, there is always one major propensity. Which is your family?

White: Anger

Anger is an aggressive energy and it can explode into harmful behavior when we don't get what we want or when someone tries to take what is ours. It is hard, sharp, and cold, like ice shards in winter. But this adamantine quality can transmute into penetrating wisdom. Wisdom cuts through delusion and we can clearly see the world around us and precisely evaluate any situation.

Yellow: Pride

"I yam what I yam," Popeye says. Pride is self-satisfied and closed off. It is constantly afraid of failing, which would undermine its carefully constructed foundation of self-possession. Pride is earthy. This richness can transform into equanimity, the understanding that whatever happens is meant to be. We are no longer threatened and so become generous with our resources.

Red: Passion

Passion thinks that it can become complete by possessing people and things. There is a sense of lacking something. "I need, I want, I cling" is passion's plaint. We no longer care about the world because we are enmeshed by selfish desire. This consuming desire burns fiery hot, but when we come to understand and embrace passion, it transmutes into the warmth of compassion.

Green: Jealousy

Jealousy and envy are symptoms of distrust in our own abilities. There is an underlying suspicion that we are not capable of succeeding; that we are not good enough. We fear that the world is against us, thwarting our every move and so we do nothing at all. It is like being trapped in a whirlwind. But the energy of the wind can transform into appropriate action. When we are not hampered by fear of failing, we are free to do the best we can and let go of the results.

Blue: Ignorance

This ignorance is one of laziness; we don't want to learn or grow because it takes too much effort. Even though our circumstances or emotions may be painful, it's easier to do nothing than struggle to change them. This slothful staying power can be transformed into the virtue of spaciousness. We are willing to perceive and embrace everything, not because we are lazy, but because we see that everything is part of us.

The transformation of these emotions comes not by trying to push them away, but by becoming more aware of them. We carefully watch them as they arise and pass away. We begin to see that

The energy in each emotion has a positive side.

One summer, I was feeling particularly annoyed at someone who was not fulfilling my expectations. The anger filled my body with tension and I couldn't sit still. Normally I would attempt to avoid the tension by vegging out, skipping from one distraction to another—television, books, magazines, food—without being able to concentrate on any one. I tried the meditation on page 45, but the anger was so strong that even though it faded, it kept coming up again. Finally, I decided to use the energy by performing a task I particularly disliked—getting down on my hands and knees to remove the weeds that had sprouted between bricks on my patio. The crevices were so narrow that I had to use a pointed screwdriver or my fingernails to dislodge the weeds. It was hot, my nails began to chip, and my knees hurt. But after a while, I relaxed into the rhythm of the work and began to notice the differences in the weeds; some leaves were round, some oval, some serrated, or pointed. There were myriad shades of green and yellow and the textures varied as well. Grass pushed up and so did tiny ferns, moss, and crawling vines. I had never noticed them before. When I finished the task, I had a sense of accomplishment and my anger had disappeared. Where had it gone? It had magically transformed into discriminating wisdom.

If you have identified one of the families: anger, pride, passion, jealousy, or ignorance as your prime energy, you can begin to befriend it by noting it when it arises. "Oh, here is my pride again." This gentle acknowledgment gives the energy the necessary space to transform. You may also want to honor the emotion by claiming its color. Wear a yellow scarf or keep yellow flowers in your house.

Guilt and Shame

Guilt is what we feel when we judge ourselves. We hold our-selves to a standard of perfection and when we fail to meet our expectations, we beat ourselves up. Shame is what we feel when we believe we have not lived up to others' expectations. Sometimes the standards are instilled by our culture or reli-gion; sometimes by our parents and friends.

> *Guilt is what we feel when we judge ourselves;*
> *Shame is what we feel when we believe we*
> *have not lived up to others' expectations.*
> *Come back to your center by acknowledging*
> *your positive qualities.*

As a child, when I first was allowed to go to confession, I would have to dredge up all my bad habits. At ten years of age, how many sins could I have committed? By focusing on my faults, I was practicing a life-long pattern of ignoring my virtues. Many of us became entangled in the same self-abne-gating habit, unbalancing our self-esteem. Come back to your center by acknowledging your positive qualities.

❀ Practice: Finding Balance ❀

Write down something you feel guilt or shame about.

What caused you to perform the harmful action: greed/desire, anger/aversion, ignorance, fear?

How did your emotion manifest: killing, lying, stealing, promiscuity, cheating, speaking ill of others?

Now write down all the times you can remember that you acted in the opposite, positive way.

If you lied, write down the times you told the truth, even though it was difficult.

If you stole or cheated, list the times you were generous with time, money, or talents.

If you slandered someone, remember each instance you used kind speech.

Recognize that you are capable of harm and equally capable of good.

May I love myself exactly as I am.
May I be happy with things just as they are.

By acknowledging what we have done and discovering what we are capable of achieving, we can let go of guilt and shame. By cultivating the inherent good in ourselves, we can transform the way we live in the world. It is possible to develop good habits.

Because I am so critical of myself, I tend to be critical of others, and I'm not shy about voicing my disapproval. Over the years, it has become a habit and even if I've learned to hold my tongue sometimes, I slip just as often. Even if my judgment is not voiced, it is intoned loud and clear in my head. Several people have brought this inclination to my attention, but it took my own careful observation to realize that it was there. It took mindfulness to notice why I needed to constantly judge and compare. For a time I was vigilant about not voicing disapproval and then I had an "Aha!" moment when it became clear that I could cultivate the equal, but opposite action—kind speech. Whenever I notice that someone has done a good job, or looks particularly nice, now I make an effort to tell them.

After a long day training to be chaplains at a city hospital, a fellow student and I were walking uptown. Although we were both weary from being on our feet all day and listening to countless sad stories, we knew the walk would help ease our tension and clear our heads. A young man approached us asking for a subway token. He related a sad story about rushing from his school in Brooklyn to visit a sick relative and leaving his wallet behind. I gave him a token. Carol berated me because she said it was probably a con and I was a fool to give away money. She said that she never gave money to panhandlers or the homeless because they use it for alcohol and drugs. At first, I was judgmental of her; after all, she was a seminary student with a desire to work with people who were ill and dying. Aren't we all worthy of care? Then I realized that I avoided the homeless, too. It was painful for me to see them; perhaps they reminded me of the precarious state that is our life. Everything changes, and someday I could be in that situation too. I also saw that I was naturally parsimonious, not wanting to part with my money, hoarding it against some possible disaster. There and then, I decided that on the way home from the hospital, I would keep some money in my coat pocket to give to those who asked. I would not shove it at them to get rid of them, but I would look at their faces and silently send them loving-kindness: "May you be safe, happy, and peaceful, strong and healthy. I wish you well."

That winter, I began to recognize some of the homeless people on my route and to miss them when they weren't there. It also eased my relationship to money; as I became giving to others, I stopped denying myself little luxuries like a taxi ride or a new art book.

By cultivating generosity, I was able to let go of guilt about my stinginess.

Harming Yourself

We forget that

Much of the harm we experience is done by us to us

Sometimes we don't even know how we harm ourselves. A good beginning is to become conscious of thoughts, words, and actions that cause us to suffer.

Actions

When I was in the sixth grade I loved to read, but my choice of books was narrow. I usually selected historical fiction or science fiction. I felt that my life was boring and that I was boring so I looked for excitement in the past and future. This addiction was pretty tame, but it set the tone for the rest of my life. I was always looking for some place outside myself for a sense of excitement and validation.

For many of us, compulsive habits are a means of escape from a painful or boring existence. We fantasize, watch too much television, or surf the net. We may then use alcohol, drugs, or food to deaden the pain. Others create a fleeting adrenalin rush by taking unnecessary risks or seeking danger. We feel like victims and our only sense of control is to monitor food intake or obsessively over-exercise.

When we fear the outside world, we oversleep and isolate ourselves to such a degree that we won't leave the house. When we fear that we are not as good as everyone else then we avoid social situations and retreat into a cocoon of self-pity.

Sometimes our self-esteem is so low that we damage our health by smoking or eating unhealthy food. We may neglect to have annual checkups at the doctor, or refuse to take prescribed medication.

When things are going well, we just can't accept that we are worthy and sabotage our jobs or relationships. I have a friend who has had many jobs. Each time it looks as if he'll succeed or be promoted, he decides that he's bored, but he isn't able to resign. His ploy is to become so obnoxious at work that he's fired. This is a recurring pattern in his life.

Another acquaintance relocates at the drop of a hat. If she has lots of friends and a satisfying job, she absconds. If she's lonely and bored, she moves to another state. She's like Goldilocks looking for the chair, food, bed that is just right, not realizing that the feeling of "just right" is within herself.

Sylvia is petrified of failing and equally terrified of succeeding. She takes on big projects, but rarely finishes them, which only deepens her self-hatred.

All of these harmful actions stem from fear and self-loathing.

❧ Practice: Forgiving Our Self-Harming Actions ❧

Take paper and pencil and find a quiet, comfortable place to sit. First center yourself by watching your breath going in and out and feeling you chest or abdomen rising and falling.

When you are ready, write down some of your habits that are harmful to yourself. Phrase them this way: I… (for example, "I drink too much.")

Usually we know what they are, but writing them down makes them more real.

Don't go overboard—two or three are enough.

Take responsibility for your actions by reading the sentences aloud.

Now sit silently for a few moments, watching your breath. When you're ready, ask yourself why you do what you do. An answer may not come to you right away, but if it does then write it by phrasing it in this way:

When I'm feeling unloved, I eat too much.
When I'm fearful, I drink too much.
When I'm bored, I seek danger.
When I'm anxious, I bite my nails.

Now read the sentences aloud. How do you feel when you voice what you've written?

Write down your feeling, using these as examples:

I am ashamed that I drink too much when I'm afraid.
I hate myself when I overeat because I feel lonely.

Now that your secret is out in the open, it's time to release the shame.

Find a comfortable place to sit or lie down. Take a couple of really deep breaths, being aware of your breath going in and out and feeling your chest and abdomen rise and fall.

Now do a body scan, asking each part of your body to relax. Start at the top of your head and move through your face, neck, shoulders, arms, hands, your torso, ending with your feet. You can go quickly or slowly, visualizing as much detail as you wish. Remember to keep the awareness of the breath within reach.

If you come to a part of the body that is very tight or painful, then give it extra attention. This may be where the shame and guilt reside. Place your hand on that part of the body and wish it well.

May you be relaxed and comforted.
May all pain and tension be released.
May my body be peaceful and serene.

As you notice the discomfort easing, continue scanning the rest of your body.

When you get to your feet, then visualize all the shame and guilt leaving your body through the tips of your toes.

Continue to follow your breath as your rest in a state of

relaxation.

Whenever the feeling of guilt and shame arise, then do the body scan.

Words and Thoughts

If other people don't put us down, then we'll do it for them. Someone pays you a compliment on a new outfit and you demur, "Oh, I got it on sale." You complete a difficult task at work, your boss acknowledges your effort, and you reply, "It was nothing." You trip on something, drop a package, and exclaim, "I'm so clumsy."

When I was a child, I remember chanting, "Sticks and stones may break my bones, but words can never harm me." Not true! The words we heard when we were young become entrenched in our memory, and when similar situations occur, we echo the words.

When I was in the fifth grade at St. Sylvester's, I sat next to Charlie Ambrosio. He had a great voice, and whenever there was a school play or parents day, he was always chosen to sing a solo. Charlie could hold notes for a very long time, adding drama to the most mundane song and he fancied himself a budding Tony Bennett. In those days, the Catholic mass was sung in Gregorian chant, and I loved singing in the choir. Although I never learned to read regular music, I excelled at deciphering the punctums and podatums on the Gregorian staff. I sang out, loud and clear, but perhaps not always so melodiously. Charlie would poke me in the side and tell me to shut up because I couldn't sing. Even in class, when we sang the "Star-Spangled Banner" each morning, he'd chortle at my singing voice. Eventually I became so self-conscious, that I wouldn't sing at all; I'd just mouth the words. That year, as part of our music exam, each student had to stand in front of the class and sing part of a song. When it was my turn I reluctantly stood up, but I could not summon the courage to sing. I stalled. Sister Rose Ann gave me some gentle encouragement, but eventually lost her patience and demanded that I begin. I balked and refused to sing. Finally, I was told to sit down and I failed my music exam. It was the only time I ever failed a school subject.

For the rest of my life I avoided music, believing I had a tin ear. Charlie's words had become my words, "I can't sing." I detested parties where people would sing together, because I believed that everyone would laugh at me. My phobia about music burgeoned into dislike and I never played music at home, preferring silence.

Forty years later, I was in training to be a monk and had to learn to perform all the jobs at a Zendo: cleaning the incense bowls, setting up the altar, sounding the instruments, and finally, leading the chants during service. I was shaking in my boots. There were several people who had great voices (like Charlie), but everyone had to take a turn. I practiced at home for days before my debut, and in the car beforehand. By the time the ceremony began, my voice was gone and it cracked at crucial times during the service. But I doggedly turned up each Saturday to embarrass myself. One day, I chanted totally in tune and that changed everything. From then on, I enjoyed group singing and chanting. I began to sing while I was taking a shower, and even if I was out of tune, I no longer cared.

The words that Charlie had carelessly uttered had become my words and as a result, I closed the door to an entire dimension of life and enjoyment. Charlie still lives in my parents' neighborhood and I ran into him one day. He admitted he had had a crush on me and his teasing was a way of making me pay attention to him!

❀ Practice: Forgiving Our Self-Harming Thoughts ❀

Write down some words and sentences that have harmed you.

Phrase them this way: "Someone said I _____
when I _____." For example: "My sister always said I was
dumb when I didn't agree with her."

Now write down the ways you have made the words your
own:

> *"I can't voice my opinions, because I'm not as smart as other
> people." ("I'm dumb")*
>
> *"I can't go to graduate school because I'll fail the entrance
> exam." (I'm dumb.")*
>
> *"I'll never be able to travel because I'm won't be able to
> exchange money."(I'm dumb.")*
>
> *"I don't deserve a promotion, because I'm not as sharp as
> everyone else." (I'm dumb.")*

Find a quiet spot and begin to watch your breath. When
you are centered, imagine that the person who first uttered
the harmful words is sitting in front of you.

Ask her why she said what she did. "Why did you say I was
dumb?"

Return to watching your breath until an answer arises.
"You were dumb."

If the answer is not satisfactory, ask her again. "Why did
you say I was dumb?"

Sit quietly until she answers. "You never agree with me."

Ask her, "Why did you think I had to agree with you?"

Wait for her answer. "I didn't trust my own opinions and
when you didn't agree with me I wanted to make myself feel
better."

Continue the dialogue until you find the motivation. You
may discover that the words are not true, they simply came
out of jealousy, anger, frustration, or loneliness. The judg-

ment may have no basis in fact.

Can you change your words now?

"Just because I don't agree with everyone doesn't mean I'm dumb."

"My opinions are worthwhile and valid."

"If I fail at one thing, it doesn't mean that I'll fail at everything."

Then there are the thoughts that wound our self-esteem. "I can't" and "I should" are lethal weapons. Disarm them. When we intuitively understand that there is a true self that is perfect and complete exactly as it is, then we are free from fear. We do the best we can and let go of the results.

I tend to be a perfectionist and take pride in what I do. Unfortunately, this sometimes keeps me from trying new things, because I want do things well. While I resided at a monastery, I sometimes was called upon to help in the kitchen. Although I like to eat, I don't enjoy preparing food, and am not a good cook. Usually I was just a helper, chopping vegetables or washing salad greens. After lunch on a Friday, the work assignments were announced. My name was called for kitchen duty and I waited to see who would be in charge. No other name was called. Uh oh! It must be a mistake, I thought. Nope. The chief cook had to leave for the weekend and it was up to me to prepare dinner, not just for the usual twenty or so residents, but for the forty people due for the weekend retreat. I was given recipes and got to work. As people filtered through the kitchen (usually to cadge a cookie or treat), they began to notice that I was calm and capable. It was simply exhaustion and shock. I prepared the meal for sixty—soup, salad, and sesame noodles. I even had time to make cookies for the next day. I began to see that doing the best I could was enough. The results were not up to me. The meal was a success, many people congratulated me, and I felt proud of my accomplishment and looked forward to the next day. At work practice meeting the next morning, someone else was assigned to be head cook and I was demoted to chopping and washing. So I learned another lesson: pride in accomplishment is extra.

Sometimes the words we don't say harm us as well. You are at an important business meeting and you disagree with the group, but are afraid to voice dissent. Someone is putting you down and you don't stand up for yourself. A person harasses you at work and you fail to report him. Underneath this self-abnegation is the false belief that we are not worthy.

We don't have to perform to a set standard to deserve love and respect. We don't have to be especially handsome or smart or successful or talented or rich.

Love is our birthright.

It's time to forgive yourself.

🌸 Practice: Loving-Kindness and Forgiveness 🌸

Find a quiet place and sit in a comfortable position. Begin by placing all of your attention on your breath. Notice the inhalation and the exhalation. You may notice that there is a space between an exhalation and the next inhalation.

Begin by calling to mind your own image. If you cannot visualize yourself, then connect with yourself by using your name. Begin by saying the loving-kindness phrases:

May I be safe from inner and outer harm.
May I be happy and peaceful.
May I be strong and healthy.

May I take care of myself with joy.

Just keep repeating the phrases, trying to arouse the feeling of unconditional love. If you sense resistance, then begin the forgiveness practice:

*For all the harm I have done to others, knowingly or
    unknowingly, I forgive myself.*
*For all the harm others have done to me, knowingly or
    unknowingly, I forgive you as much as I can.*
*For all the harm I have done myself, knowingly or
    unknowingly, I forgive myself.*
May I be safe from harm.
May I be happy and peaceful.
May I be strong and healthy.
May I take care of myself with joy.

Continue to repeat the phrases until they fall away and you are basking in serenity.

You can use this meditation every day. Decide in advance how long you would like to sit and continue even if you feel distracted or agitated. You may not experience loving-kindness at first, but you are watering the seed—gradually the loving-kindness blossoms. Metta meditation can set the tone for the day and for your life. When you begin with a loving intention, there is the likelihood of its continuing through the day and spilling out to others. Like loving-kindness, forgiveness begins with oneself. It can radiate throughout our lives, opening our hearts to be able to forgive others.

When we have an open heart and mind, then we can forgive anything, anyone, and even ourselves. We can view each moment with fresh eyes, not clouded by fear or expectation, and act free from judging and comparing. An open heart is an accepting heart.

❋ 5 ❋

Circle of Forgiveness

Forgiveness is not just an occasional act;
it is a permanent attitude.
—Martin Luther King, Jr.

When I went to say goodbye to my dying father, I wanted to tell him how he had ignored me during my childhood and how worthless it made me feel. We had never been able to have this kind of discussion before and I wanted to seize my last chance to have him acknowledge the harm he had caused me, because I believed that I would be able to release the lingering resentment that tainted every relationship I tried to form. I would be able to forgive him and get on with my life. But he looked so wizened and vulnerable in his hospital bed, gasping oxygen through the ventilator, that I hesitated.

This was not what he had planned. He wanted to stay home, making believe that everything would be okay. He was in this predicament because he had avoided going to the doctor when his habitual morning cough became hacking and lasted throughout the day and the family became alarmed at his extreme weight loss. By the time he agreed to see a doctor the tumor in his lung was inoperable. He refused treatment and stayed at home. When he collapsed one Sunday, I drove home and insisted that he be taken to the hospital. My mother was near exhaustion from coaxing him to eat and helping him dress, and I worried that she could not handle his dying at home. So, against his will, my father was carried out to an ambulance and, in transit, had a heart attack.

At the hospital, he was intubated and as he lay in the emergency room, his eyes begged me for help. I was wracked by guilt because I believed that I was the cause of his suffering and was powerless to end it.

So here I was, standing awkwardly at his deathbed, thinking of my needs. Finally, my heart opened and I took his hand in mine and told him that I loved him, and I meant it. A lifetime of resentments, large and small, finally had transformed into love. And if he wanted to say, "I love you too," he couldn't, because he had no voice left. It didn't matter, because my love was not conditioned on his being or acting according to my expectations. It was enough that I forgave him for any harm he had inflicted, knowingly or unknowingly.

So here we are, back at the beginning.

Forgiveness is the final form of love.

But that is not the end of the story. Although I believed I had put down my bundle of resentments, I was blissfully unaware that I needed my father's forgiveness for the harm I had caused him at the end of his life. The need haunted me for several months, although it was so shadowy that I could not readily identify what was at the bottom of my unease.

One summer, during a workshop, the leader suggested that if we had any unfinished business, we could resolve it by writing letters to and from the person who had died. The exercise helped me to understand my father's point of view and some of his own hopes and fears. We were able to come to a meeting of minds and hearts and I was able to extend forgiveness to my father, accept his forgiveness, and be freed from guilt. I was able to forgive myself. When you are ready, you may want to try the following practice in reconciliation.

❋ Practice: Letters of Reconciliation ❋

Allow at least a couple of hours of quiet time to complete this exercise, and find a place where you won't be disturbed by visitors or phone calls. Have a pad of paper and pen readily available. Sit comfortably and place an empty chair in front of you.

Close your eyes and take several deep breaths, and then call to mind the person to whom you wish to write. Imagine her or him in detail: facial expression, posture, and clothing, and see the person sitting in the chair in front of you.

Then open your eyes and begin to write a letter to that person. Tell her or him your feelings and thoughts about the situation between you. Don't hold anything back and don't censor angry or bitter words. When you have finished, remind yourself of the person's image in the chair and read the letter aloud to her or him.

Let the words sink in and then move to the other chair. Put yourself in the other person's position. How do you feel when you hear the letter? Take a couple of deep, cleansing breaths, and then begin to write a response. Describe how you (as the other person) feel now and explain why you may have caused harm. Then read the letter aloud.

Move back to your own chair and reflect on the letter your friend wrote. How do you feel now? Do the words make you angrier or do you begin to understand the person's point of view? Respond to the letter, and then read it aloud.

Write letters back and forth until an understanding has been reached.

If you feel the air has been cleared, then imagine the person getting up and leaving you. Wave goodbye and wish the person well.

You may have to do this exercise several times before you understand that the other person could not have acted otherwise, even as you could not have reacted differently. But everything changes and grows and it's time to let go and move on.

Renewing Relationships

When we try to resolve differences with a living person, we realize that, in retrospect, it was easier to reconcile with a dead person. During the letter-writing exercise, although we tried to put ourselves in the other person's shoes, we still projected our personal beliefs on him. Healing a relationship with living beings requires more work because they are not so compliant. They may not respond the way we'd like or expect. Forgiving and apologetic words are only the first step. It is an attitude of acceptance that allows a faltering relationship to become stronger. Try this meditation to let go.

> *An attitude of acceptance allows a faltering relationship to become stronger.*

🌸 Practice: Let Go 🌸

Sit in a comfortable position, close your eyes, and for a few moments focus on the sensation of your breath going in and out.

Call to mind the situation that has caused you pain. Don't worry about the other person or the details of the story. Concentrate on the distress you feel. Can you locate it in your body?

Visualize the sensation as a beautiful bird trapped in your chest or heart or stomach (wherever the suffering resides). The bird is frightened and beats its wings, trying to escape its prison. Send the bird compassion.

May your distress be eased.
May you experience acceptance and serenity.
May you be released from suffering.

Continue repeating the phrases for some time, and when you are ready, imagine that the bird has ceased struggling and, in that moment of surrender, an opening occurs. Then hold the image of the bird, soaring through the sky and clouds, graceful, and free.

Call up that wonderful feeling of release whenever you meet the person with whom you have difficulty. It may help to visualize two birds swirling and flying through the air—the other person has his or her own distress, too.

Whenever the memory of the tension between the two of you surfaces, take a couple of deep breaths and silently say:

You are a being just like myself.
As I desire freedom from suffering, so do you.
As I desire serenity, so do you.
May you be well.

If you feel uncomfortable around the person, then silently repeat the phrases before you speak to him.

In the Zen tradition, the phrase "beginner's mind" denotes the highest form of attainment. It means that we greet each situation, person, and moment as if it were the first time we experienced them. Every meeting is fresh and new, untainted by previous thoughts or feelings. Imagine how freeing it would be if we were able to put aside our resentments and start each relationship anew. It's possible, but it takes practice. It helps when we realize that there is a thread that binds us all and that we all yearn to be happy and free.

The Truth of Existence

When you look at snowflakes through a microscope, each one is unique, but they are all snow.

Sometimes it takes a dramatic event to wake us up to the fact that we are all connected, and that in spite of the differences between us, we all share the same inherent nature.

For me, it was my father's death; for others, it is a near-death experience, an ecstatic spiritual vision, or witnessing a tragedy. We then discover what the Buddha discovered 2,500 years ago when he saw the morning star—the three characteristics of existence: suffering, impermanence, and selflessness.

Suffering

Dhukka, a word in the Pali language, is usually translated as "suffering," but the actual meaning is closer to inherently unsatisfactory. We may think that we only suffer occasionally, but everything is unsatisfactory in some way. You may achieve your fondest desire, but there's a niggling worry that it will disappear.

During a mindfulness workshop for cancer patients, I passed around a basket of peanut M&M's, and asked each person to take one and hold it. I instructed them to wait until everyone had a candy, but some people were chomping at the bit and wanted to eat their M&M right away. Imagine that you had been in the audience. After looking at the M&M, enjoying the color, and feeling the smoothness in your hand,

I asked you to eat the candy, not gobbling it up, but savoring the brittle crust, the melting chocolate, and the surprise of the hard nut at the heart of the candy.

The M&M was delicious, but then it was gone and you might have missed it. That's suffering. You could be allergic to chocolate and couldn't participate in the exercise, so you felt left out—suffering. If you thought about spoiling your appetite for lunch or worried about going off your diet, that's suffering. You might have thought that the exercise was stupid and were annoyed at having to participate—suffering.

When I passed around the basket, it took forever, because people were looking for their favorite color, and if they couldn't find it they were unhappy. Why? All the candy tasted the same. It is our propensity to pick and choose, to form opinions and judgments that causes suffering. So even something as insignificant as a piece of candy can cause suffering.

Even when we get what we want we cling to it, wanting it to stay the same. I have a friend, Karen, who loves her children deeply. She struggles to protect them from every possible danger. A few weeks after the September 11 tragedy, her 10 year-old son was to fly cross-country for an annual visit with his uncle. Karen was sick to her stomach and couldn't sleep for several days prior to the flight. She struggled with her desire to protect her child, telling him not to go, but also not wanting to instill fear in him. Finally, she decided to allow him to take the trip, but she could not see him off at the airport because she knew her tears and nervousness would upset him. Her love is a double-edged sword, bringing her great joy, but also causing her equally great suffering.

Impermanence
Everything changes. Look at nature: night becomes day; the seasons change; flowers bud, blossom, go to seed, and then

fade away. Like us: we are born, grow up, age, get sick, die, and, some believe, are reborn. We like to think that things are solid and will last forever. If you really liked that M&M, you might have clutched it in your hand, saving it for later. But eventually it would have melted.

When we fall in love, we believe it is everlasting, but the divorce rate shows that this isn't so. Our ideas and opinions change as well; one year you may love reality TV shows, the next they seem irrelevant. Cells in our body are dying and being replenished even as you read this page. To explore the changing nature of reality, try the following practice.

❀ Practice: Observing Impermanence and Cherishing the Moment ❀

Sit in a meditation posture that's comfortable for you and close your eyes. Begin to watch your breath, noting the inhalation, the exhalation and the space between the out-breath and the next in-breath. Explore the quality of the breath, noticing whether it is ragged or smooth, deep or shallow, easy or forced. Is the inhalation the same length as the exhalation? Which one is longer?

As you relax into the rhythm of the breath, open to the sounds around you. Do not try to identify what they are, or whether they are pleasant or annoying. It doesn't make any difference whether you hear a bird, a snippet of conversation, traffic, or the radiator clanking. Simply listen, placing all your attention on sound arising, then passing away.

Notice how a sound may pop up suddenly, startling you, or sneak into your consciousness slowly, coming nearer and nearer, becoming stronger and stronger until it begins to drift away and fade.

Make a note that as sound arises and passes away, so to all

existence must arise and pass away as well. All of our thoughts and emotions are ephemeral. All that has been created in nature will change and all that humans have created will change as well.

Return to the sensation of the breath going in and out. Place all of your attention on your breath, knowing that it is happening in the present moment and that's all we can rely on. The present moment is a perfect moment. It is all of eternity.

Selflessness

What makes up "you"? In an earlier chapter, you might have discovered that you are not your name, your profession, your relationships, your possessions, or your body. The holy grail of many spiritual practices is to find out "Who am I and why am I here?" If you did the meditation practice I suggested, you may have intuited that you are nobody and everybody, all at the same time. Even though we come in different sizes, shapes, and colors, even if we have different languages, beliefs, and cultures, there is a universal life force that we all share. Not only are we part of the whole, we *are* the whole—the universe in a grain of sand. We are one body.

It isn't enough to intellectually grasp the concepts of suffering, impermanence, and selflessness. It is necessary to directly experience their truth—to *be* suffering, to *be* impermanence, to *be* selfless. The events of September 11 have presented many of us with that opportunity. In our own backyard, we saw that nothing lasts forever: monumental buildings, financial security, jobs, relationships—gone in a flash—impermanence. We have suffered by losing friends and grieve for people we never knew. We have lived in paralyzing fear for our safety—suffering.

We have directly experienced the
truth of the oneness of all beings:
When one person is harmed, all of us are harmed.

Many of us have transformed grief, anger, and fear into generosity, helping our neighbors, and reaching out to the perceived enemy by feeding the hungry in Afghanistan. When you are hungry, my stomach growls.

We have the opportunity to make a fresh start. The best way to avoid needing to seek forgiveness or to offer it is to nurture the part of us that naturally leans toward performing acts of kindness, so that no harmful actions are committed. Remember this quote?

> *As a mother would risk her life to protect her child, her only*
> *child,*
> *Even so should one cultivate a boundless heart with regard to*
> *all beings.*

Cultivating a Boundless Heart

A closed heart can be pried open a bit by admitting that we have caused harm. Forgiveness and atonement open it further, and vowing not to cause suffering in the future continues the healing.

To achieve a boundless heart means going
a step further, deciding to live our lives
from a place of wisdom and compassion.
We not only vow not to cause suffering,
but to alleviate it when we encounter it.

Avoiding Harm

We have already looked at desire, attachment, and ignorance, the causes of harm.

Mindfulness is the tool that helps us to avoid causing suffering. Keep it sharp!

It is helpful to meditate each day because it hones our awareness. At first, we notice the nuances of our breath and then we open to the sounds around us, our bodily sensations, and emotions. This alertness seeps into our daily life and we become attuned to the subtleties of human interaction. We begin to sense what is said and what is left unsaid and this understanding helps us to avoid causing harm.

Our normal way of reacting or withdrawing crumbles. We are no longer prisoners of our conditioning, and we act from a clear place. We cease causing harm to ourselves and others.

Practicing Good

We're ready to take the next step and activate the kinder, gentler side of ourselves. Peter Pan taught children to fly, "Think lovely thoughts and up you'll go!" In a way, that's what we'll do.

We can nurture kindness just as we tend our gardens.

We water our thoughts with the knowledge that we are all connected, and fertilize with kind thoughts and words. Try to practice loving-kindness meditation each day, even if for a moment or two. Each time a negative thought arises, replace it with a positive thought. When someone riles you and you're tempted to react, make an effort to find something good about the person. Bring yourself back to center by taking a few deep breaths. Practicing good begins with your-self, so remember to be kind and forgiving when you don't meet your expectations.

Practicing Good for Others

We're moving into the realm of compassionate action. When we see a wrong, we try to right it. When someone needs help, we offer it. We becomes generous with our resources, both material and spiritual, knowing that there is always enough to go around. There is something deeper, as well. When we act, we realize that we are acting for everyone.

True generosity is when the giver, the receiver, and the gift are empty—there is just generosity. This selfless giving flows from our essential nature where there is no expectation of approval or reward.

> *Selfless giving continues throughout all space*
> *and time, and when we practice good for*
> *others, we are practicing for ourselves as well.*

The Gifts of Forgiveness

We tend to think that forgiveness is our gift to those who have harmed us. While this is true, we sometimes forget that for-giveness is a catalyst to self-healing. Qualities that are buried under layers of resentment, shame, and guilt are revealed and the light of forgiveness nurtures them. Courage, patience, and gratitude are the gifts of forgiveness.

Courage

In order to truly understand harm, we need to look deeply into our own behavior to see how we cause suffering, and that requires courage. It takes courage to admit to ourselves that we have the same potential to cause harm as to perform good acts, and that opens the way to understand and forgive those who hurt us. It takes courage to confront a person when they have wronged us, and courage to forgive. We start with baby steps, forgiving the small stuff, and then move on to deeper hurts. It takes courage to be humble enough to admit our own mistakes and then to resolve to transform our behavior.

Finally, we forgive ourselves for not being perfect and that takes the most courage. It doesn't happen overnight, so we learn to be patient.

Patience

It is a struggle to step away from our conditioned behavior.

> *Transformation is hard work, and*
> *learning to forgive takes patience.*

We do all of the suggested exercises and meditations, but we cling to the last vestige of resentment with our fingernails. We are willing to forgive, but not yet. And that's okay. Practice being patient with yourself. Simple awareness of how we feel, without trying to deny the negative emotions helps us to ease our grip. I am willing to forgive you as much as I can. That's enough for now.

At my first important job with an educational publishing company, I was able to take pedestrian manuscripts and turn them into innovative learning tools for students. The projects made a sizeable profit and I thought I was doing a great job. Writers and illustrators enjoyed working with me, but my associates were not quite so enthralled. My focus was on producing the best learning tools and I had little patience for company policy and politics. I was proud when potential authors said I didn't sound like a company person.

One day at a celebratory dinner, I was dressed down for not being a team player and a sycophantic co-worker was appointed head of the department. She had produced nothing. I was angry that my work was not appreciated, heartbroken at being passed over, and resigned to start my own company. I was promised a large free-lance job by the editor-in-chief, but a few days before I left, the publisher reneged. At the time, I had about $500 in the bank, and because I had resigned, I was not eligible for unemployment benefits. My rage at the publisher grew exponentially, fueled by fear. Forgiveness was not even a glimmer on the horizon. I wanted payback. The best way was to make a success of my new venture. (See what you missed, you fools!) When my replacement was fired, I gloated. My dreams were rife with twisted scenarios featuring the downfall of the publisher.

After ten years or so, my anger faded, but forgiveness never entered my mind. After another fifteen years, I believed I had forgotten the entire incident, but the same story played itself out again. The actors were different, the place was not the same, but the circumstances were. I felt rejected and unappreciated, and so I resigned. The original situation surfaced from the recesses of my memory and I had an insight. Both situations were caused by the same behavior—mine. Yet again, I learned something about myself and understood that I shared responsibility for the outcome of both situations. In that moment, I was able to forgive my tormentors and, not incidentally, myself. Twenty-five years! Patience. Finally, a burr has been removed from my psyche.

Dreams of vengeance were replaced by a sense of gratitude. I realized that I never would have had the guts to leave a steady job to start my own business. The publisher had ejected me from the nest and in large measure, I had him to thank for my successful company.

Gratitude

We have practiced awareness and acceptance of ourselves and others and they have helped transform our negative energy into positive action. We become comfortable with the ways things are and gratitude is aroused. We realize that our life is a precious gift, exactly the way it is. How wonderful to be able to see the intrinsic good in all things!

Here's a Zen story:

> *A long, long time ago, in a land far, far away, there lived a man who seemed to have everything—a sturdy house, a job, and enough money to buy whatever he desired. But he was not happy. He felt empty inside and thought that if he discovered the meaning of life he would then be happy. He read all the great books in the local library but he could not find the answer. He traveled from village to village speaking to holy men and wise women, but none of their answers rang true. Then he learned about an ancient woman who lived at the top of the highest mountain in the land. Everyone said she knew the secret.*
>
> *So the man traveled for many days through forests and valleys, crossing streams and rivers, until he finally reached the mountains. He struggled up the highest peak and his excitement grew. He thought, "Soon I will have the answer; soon I will be happy!"*
>
> *When he reached the summit, he saw a crone dressed in rags, gathering firewood, her back and limbs crippled by arthritis.*
>
> *"I have journeyed a great distance and am exhausted by effort," he said. "Please tell me the meaning of life!"*

The old woman said, "Thank you very much."

"You're welcome," answered the man, thinking the old woman had not heard correctly.

"What is the meaning of life?" he shouted in her ear.

"Thank you very much," replied the woman.

Unbelieving, the man gasped, "That's it? That's all? Are you sure?"

"Thank you very much," nodded the woman.

The man didn't think it was a very good answer, but decided to give it a try. As he traveled back the way he had come, he said, "Thank you very much" to everyone he met. "Thank you very much, thank you very much, THANK YOU VERY MUCH!" But still he was not happy.

He was boiling with rage and went back to the old woman and shouted at her, "I've been saying 'Thank you very much' to everyone, but it doesn't work. I'm not happy! Please tell me the real, true secret meaning of life."

The woman beckoned him closer and said, "Thank you very much."

The moral of the story is that gratitude has to be authentic. Like forgiveness, parroting the words is not enough. When we have caused suffering for ourselves or others, we need to feel true remorse and decide not to repeat our words or actions. When someone has harmed us, we need to offer forgiveness with our whole heart and resolve to let go of resentment. Our minds and hearts have only enough space for one thing at a time.

I learned this during a retreat. I was trying to meditate, but one of my teeth had become abscessed and the ache was agonizing. I thought the throbbing would never end and gritting my teeth made it worse. Then, on the last evening, I sat down awkwardly and my groin muscle cramped. It was excruciating. But the pain in my tooth was gone. Where had it gone? I then realized that the mind can only hold one thing at a time.

Where there is hatred, resentment, vengeance, or sorrow, there is no room for gratitude. Nothing cleans out our minds and hearts like forgiveness, opening the way to receive joy. As the Zen story taught us,

An attitude of gratitude is the source of joy.

*If the only prayer you say in your whole life is
"thank you," that would be enough.*
—Meister Eckhart

**Make it a habit to start each day by saying
"Thank you very much" for the gift of life.**

When you are feeling down about your life, make a list of the things for which you are grateful.

If someone harms you, make a list of the positive things about the person and express your gratitude for them.

When a person messes up, we usually let them know about it. When they do something helpful, exciting, or creative, express your gratitude by complimenting them.

Sometimes we compare ourselves to others and feel jealous or envious when they are successful, beautiful, or clever. We can excise the envy from our hearts by practicing joy at the good fortune of others.

❦ Practice: Joyfulness for Others' Good Fortune ❦

Sit in a comfortable position and begin by watching or counting your breaths. After a time, call up the image of the person of whom you feel envious or jealous. Then extend them sympathetic joy:

May your success and good fortune continue.
Your joy is my joy.
I wish you well.

Keep repeating the phrases until you mean them. Realize that there is enough joy and good fortune in the universe for everyone and you are bound to get your share.

Completing the Circle

One of the most common Zen symbols is the *enso*, a circle. It signifies many things: emptiness, fullness, the oneness of all creations. Hundreds of calligraphers have drawn the enso, quickly sketching it with a single brushstroke. Some of the circles are delicate and spidery; some are bold and heavy. Most of the paintings are not perfect spheres, but each is a perfect reflection of the artist's mind-state. All begin and end at the same point.

We began with a handful of pewter stones—forgiveness, courage, patience, and gratitude, which inspired us to open our hearts. We end with the same qualities, but they have been amplified, because we have not only explored them, we have experienced them. Each act of forgiveness requires courage and patience. Each time we forgive strengthens the qualities and the next time is easier.

Forgiveness frees a space in our hearts for gratitude
for this precious life that we all share.

We can say, "Thank you very much," and mean it.

Peaceful Dwelling Project

Madeline Ko-i Bastis is executive director of *Peaceful Dwelling Project*, a not-for-profit organization that seeks to improve the quality of living for people with life-challenging illness and their caregivers. Peaceful Dwelling promotes the use of meditation for spiritual, emotional, and physical healing by offering workshops and retreats; training for healthcare professionals in using meditation as a complementary healing practice; and spiritual and emotional care for the dying through a volunteer network *Comfort Companions*.

There is no retreat center so we travel to your location. For more information contact:

Peaceful Dwelling Project
33 Chapel Avenue
Brookhaven, NY 11719-9401
Tel: 631-776-2444
Fax: 631-776-2442
E-mail: *info@peacefuldwelling.org*
Website: *www.peacefuldwelling.org*